West's Law School Advisory Board

PROBLEMS IN
CIVIL PROCEDURE

By

James R. Devine
Professor of Law
University of Missouri–Columbia

AMERICAN CASEBOOK SERIES®

Mat #40330339

American Casebook Series and West Group are trademarks registered in the U.S. Patent and Trademark Office.

© 2007 Thomson/West
      610 Opperman Drive
      P.O. Box 64526
      St. Paul, MN 55164–0526
      1–800–328–9352

Printed in the United States of America

ISBN–13: 978–0–314–15868–0
ISBN–10: 0–314–15868–5

TEXT IS PRINTED ON 10% POST CONSUMER RECYCLED PAPER

*To Sharon, for inspiration, for love, and for
allowing me to love the law and its processes*

*To Zach and Noah, for allowing me to
share my love of them with my profession*

*To Josh, for allowing me to share my love of
profession with him*

*To Mother, for more than I could
ever express*

*To Rachael and Christina, for the joy
they bring my sons*

To Averie, for ushering in a whole new generation

*To Neve, Dodger, and Bailey, for allowing me
to talk aloud about my writing
without verbal interruption*

PREFACE

Lawyers should help clients solve problems.

To do that, law students need to see more than just cases. In the years I have taught Civil Procedure, I have tried to use these and other problems to supplement the cases. While there is no substitute for having law students, particularly beginning law students, wrestle with the doctrine of *Pennoyer*, *Hanna*, or *Hickman*, providing context to doctrinal analysis always seems important to me. I hope these problems will help provide such context.

Problems also help assess student progress. The student who can recite a case cannot always apply the teachings of that case in a wholly independent factual setting. Hopefully, these problems will also assist that assessment.

There are not problems here for every case read or every point made in Civil Procedure. In some areas, there are probably more problems than necessary. I teach Civil Procedure pretty much in the order of this book. As a result, there are more problems in Personal and Subject Matter Jurisdiction.

I use these problems in several ways:

1. After reading and discussing a case, I will tell students to look at one of the problems and use the discussion to assess where we are;

2. Sometimes, I will assign students to play certain roles in problems. I find that doing this allows the students to live out the legal problem and develop some empathy for the circumstances–something more than a mere understanding of doctrine. I will usually ask the student playing the role of the offended party: "What do you want out of this?"

3. Students always look for practice exam questions. I sometimes use these problems for that purpose.

I am deeply indebted to all of the federal and state court judges who wrote the overwhelming majority of opinions, the facts of which I have stolen in writing this book. Editing errors are almost certainly mine.

I am also indebted to the many law students who have been subjected to various forms of most of these problems. They have helped me refine what is here.

Funding for this book comes in part from the following:

The John S. Divilbiss Faculty Research Fund,

The Charles H. Rehm Faculty Research Fellowship, and

The Stinson Morrison Hecker Faculty Research Fellowship.

I thank each of these funds for their support of legal education generally and this project specifically.

Finally, thanks go to Scott Simpson, MU School of Law, class of 2007 for his very helpful editing.

Problems are supposed to be fun to solve. Enjoy.

James R. Devine
December, 2006

Table of Contents

CHAPTER 1
PERSONAL JURISDICTION AND VENUE

CHAPTER 2
SUBJECT MATTER JURISDICTION AND REMOVAL

CHAPTER 3
ABSTENTION AND ANTI-INJUNCTION ACT

CHAPTER 4
THE ERIE DOCTRINE

CHAPTER 5
PLEADINGS AND MOTIONS

CHAPTER 6
JOINDER, INTERVENTION, SUBSTITUTION, INTERPLEADER, CLASS ACTIONS

CHAPTER 7
DISCOVERY

CHAPTER 8
RESOLUTION PRIOR TO TRIAL

CHAPTER 9
THE PROCEDURE OF TRIALS

CHAPTER 10
DEALING WITH JUDGMENTS

CHAPTER 11
APPEALS

PROBLEMS IN
CIVIL PROCEDURE

CHAPTER 1

PERSONAL JURISDICTION AND VENUE

Pennoyer and its Teaching--Introduction

Epstein v. Kantwell

Following his graduation from college, Josh Kantwell, a citizen of West Virginia, wanted to get involved in the political process. From West Virginia, Josh drove to Washington, D.C. to become a non-paid intern with a West Virginia member of Congress while he looked for full-time employment. While in D.C., Josh retained his West Virginia driver's license and automobile registration. He anticipated remaining in the district for a couple of years, but knew that eventually, he would return to West Virginia. He rented an apartment in the district at the rate of $1,500 per month from Anita Epstein. Josh had no luck at finding a job and, after six months, moved back home in West Virginia. At the time he returned home, Josh had not paid his landlord any money, other than the initial deposit, and was $7,500 behind in the rent.

Questions

1. Josh's D.C. landlord is upset that Josh moved back to West Virginia owing $7,500 rent and wants you, as Anita Epstein's lawyer, to go into court in the District of Columbia and get a judgment against Josh. Based only on your study of *Pennoyer*, how can you help your client bring Josh into court in D.C.?
2. Suppose the landlord is so upset that she is willing to bring suit in state court in West Virginia. Can the landlord go to West Virginia and file suit? How will the West Virginia court have personal jurisdiction over the landlord, who has no other business in West Virginia and who is a citizen of Washington, D.C.?

Kerr v. Merriam

Lorraine Kerr is a licensed attorney and citizen of Missouri. Kerr was contacted by Nora Merriam, a citizen of the neighboring state of Kansas. Nora had inherited real estate from her sister, who had moved from Kansas to Missouri as a child. That property was in Boone County, in central Missouri. After Nora received a valid deed to it, Nora learned that a tree on the property had fallen across the property line onto the property of Nora's neighbor, Alfred Englebloom. The tree had struck an electric generator on Englebloom's property, which had caused a fire and resulting property damage to Englebloom's land. Nora told attorney Kerr: "I want you to represent me in dealing with this tree situation. I will not come to Missouri and so I don't want to be sued there. Do whatever you need to do to settle the matter and I'll send you a check when you work out an amount I owe Englebloom. Please send your retainer agreement to me here in Kansas and I'll sign it." Kerr agreed, but asked Nora to have her signature notarized because Kerr did not know Nora and would therefore have no idea if the signature Kerr might receive would be valid. Kerr did receive a signed retainer agreement from Nora, which had been notarized according to Kansas law. Kerr also settled the damage claim with Englebloom and received a check from

Nora in the appropriate amount. When Kerr then sent a bill for legal services to Nora, Kerr was surprised when Nora refused to pay. Kerr then filed suit against Nora in the appropriate trial court in Missouri seeking payment of her $2,500 fee. Nora specially appeared in Missouri to challenge personal jurisdiction in Missouri. At the hearing on Nora's challenge, Kerr asserts that personal jurisdiction is proper, based primarily on Nora's ownership of real estate in Boone County.

Questions

1. How is this case different from *Pennoyer*?
2. If it is not different, and using only *Pennoyer* as a guide, can Kerr sue Nora in state court in Missouri?
3. Assume that Kerr's retainer agreement stated that Nora's signature on the contract constituted her appointment of Kerr's secretary as Nora's agent for purpose of accepting service over any matter related to the contract. Also assume that the State of Missouri has not authorized, by statute or judicial decision, the appointment of such agents for service. Following receipt of the lawsuit against her by Kerr, through Kerr's secretary, Nora goes to the Missouri court and files an answer denying that she owes any money to Kerr. Thereafter, Nora seeks to dismiss the entire matter, claiming an absence of personal jurisdiction. *Pennoyer* mentions just such agents for service of process and indicates that if the state has authorized them, the Court would probably accept any resulting personal jurisdiction. It follows that if the state does not have such a statutory framework, the state should not accept personal jurisdiction. Why will that reasoning not work in this problem?

City of Jamestown v. Waldron

The City of Jamestown, New York had a problem. In its downtown area was a series of three stores all part of the same older building. Each of the stores was rented to a separate tenant. The building itself was in deteriorating condition and a number of complaints about the building and its surroundings had come into city hall. When city building inspectors traced ownership of the building, they found that the owners were Howard and Rosemary Waldron, citizens of Clarion, Pennsylvania.

After further inspection, Jamestown's building inspectors found that the interior of the building was so far in violation of the City Building Code that it had to order the tenants out of the building. It then filed an action in state court in Jamestown, New York, against Howard and Rosemary Waldron seeking both a declaration that the building was a public nuisance and an order compelling the owners to remove the offending building.

Howard and Rosemary Waldron appeared for the limited purpose of contesting personal jurisdiction in New York and produced evidence that they were citizens of Pennsylvania and had all their business and personal interests in that state–although they conceded ownership of the New York building.

Question

Based only on *Pennoyer*, how should the court rule on the Waldron's motion to dismiss for want of personal jurisdiction?

The Relationship among the Parties, the Forum and the Law
Minimum Contacts/Purposeful Availment

DeVito v. Lake Wales College

Lake Wales College is a relatively small, liberal arts college in Lake Wales, Nebraska and is a corporate citizen of Nebraska. The college has its main campus in Nebraska, but also offers degrees at satellite campuses in 23 different states. Some of these satellite campuses are no more than a storefront office, where students go and watch live video of classes actually being held in Nebraska. One such state is Montana, where Lake Wales College maintains two storefront offices. In both of them, Lake Wales College students pay their fees, then sit in the store and watch live video of classes held in Nebraska. They take their tests in the stores in Montana and the tests are sent to Lake Wales, Nebraska for grading. All told, there are approximately 75 Montana residents taking Lake Wales College classes in Montana. On its main campus in Nebraska, Lake Wales College has hired the DeVito plumbing company to do regular plumbing work. After one such job, Lake Wales College did not pay DeVito. DeVito moved to Montana before realizing there was no payment and, after arriving in Montana, DeVito sued Lake Wales College in Montana state court over the non-paid plumbing bill.

Questions

1. Assuming there is proper service on the college, state as succinctly as possible, the issue the court will have to resolve if Lake Wales College moves to dismiss the state court proceeding because of an absence of personal jurisdiction.

2. How will your issue be resolved by the court? Why?

Marquard Yachts, Inc. v. Desmond Yachts, Inc.

Marquard Yachts is a New Jersey corporation with its principal offices in South Little Egg Harbor, New Jersey. Marquard Yachts designs, manufactures, markets and sells "Seaworthy Double Cabin" brand yachts.

Desmond Yachts Inc. is a Mississippi corporation with its principal offices in Gulfport, Mississippi. Desmond Yachts also sells and markets boats, but has no offices or agents in New Jersey.

Some time ago, Marquard Yachts and Desmond Yachts began negotiating a deal that was intended to allow Desmond to become the exclusive marketing representatives and dealers for Marquard's Seaworthy Double Cabin Yachts on the Gulf coast. To that end, Desmond's agents made phone calls from their offices in Mississippi to Marquard Yacht's offices in New Jersey. Additionally, Desmond transmitted facsimiles into New Jersey, including proposed licensing agreements for the trade names relevant to the negotiations. The president of Desmond also traveled to Marquard Yachts' offices in New Jersey. During one of these trips, Donald Marquard, the president of Marquard Yacht, provided the Desmond president with a copy of Marquard Yachts' sales brochure. That brochure included photographs and floor plans of the Seaworthy Yachts. Marquard Yachts also arranged and paid for Desmond's president to travel to China to observe the manufacturing process for the Seaworthy Yachts and meet Marquard Yacht's business contacts relevant to those yachts. In connection with this trip, Desmond employees sent facsimile transmissions to Donald Marquard as part of the planning activities for the China trip.

Eventually, the negotiations between the parties reached a standstill and they failed to reach an agreement. Marquard Yachts now alleges that Desmond misappropriated the photographs and floor plans contained in Marquard Yacht's sales brochure, as well as other intellectual property owned by Marquard Yachts, and used it to produce and market boats that are identical to the Seaworthy Yachts. It further alleges that Desmond engaged Marquard Yachts' business contacts in China to manufacture the boats, and thereby interfered with Marquard Yacht's business relationship with those contacts. Based on these allegations, Marquard Yacht sued Desmond Yachts, Inc., in the United States District Court for the District of New Jersey for damages.

Desmond makes a special appearance in the New Jersey court and moves to dismiss for want of personal jurisdiction.

Question

1. Marquard argues that there are sufficient "contacts" to establish personal jurisdiction. Analyze this argument.

Lorelei Equipment Manufacturing Co., Inc. v. DiNato Concrete Co., Inc.

DiNato Concrete Company, Inc., is a Missouri corporation. It does regular construction business in Missouri, Arkansas, Tennessee and Iowa. For purposes of this problem, please assume that under Illinois law, a foreign corporation must obtain a certificate of authority to do business and appoint a registered agent within the state. About eight years ago, DiNato wanted to expand its business into Illinois and, as a result, DiNato put in a successful bid to build two roads in Southern Illinois near Carbondale. To build these roads, DiNato obtained an Illinois certificate of authority and appointed a registered agent within the state. The registered agent was actually a paralegal in an attorney's office in Carbondale who regularly served as the registered agent for any corporation registered in the state by her attorney boss.

Last year, DiNato Concrete needed to purchase some machinery and did so buying this machinery from Lorelei Equipment Manufacturing Company, Inc., an Illinois corporation with a principal place of business in Lake Geneva, in northern Illinois. This purchase price of $500,000 was confirmed in a written contract indicating that any interpretation questions relating to it would be resolved "under the law of Illinois." During the manufacturing process, there were numerous telephone calls between Lorelei supervisors and DiNato employees over minor details of the manufacturing process and, on one occasion, several DiNato employees stopped at the Lorelei plant to inspect the equipment, telling the Lorelei employees they were on their way to a meeting in Milwaukee. The equipment was shipped to DiNato's principal office just outside St. Louis. DiNato Concrete then refused to pay the full purchase price of the equipment. Thereafter, Lorelei Equipment sued for the balance of the purchase price in federal court in the Southern District of Illinois in Carbondale and served the still-existing registered agent in Carbondale, Illinois. DiNato Concrete, through its attorney, filed a motion to dismiss for want of personal jurisdiction.

Questions

1. Based on your reading primarily of *International Shoe*, what is the importance of the fact that DiNato had a "registered agent" in Carbondale?

2. Does that agent establish the kinds of "contacts" needed by *International Shoe* for the transaction that is the subject of the current suit?

3. What are the "contacts" that would tend to establish personal jurisdiction for the transaction that is the subject of the current suit?

4. Are any such "contacts" sufficient to establish personal jurisdiction in Illinois? Why or why not?

Nowak v. Tak How Corporation

Tak How is a Hong Kong corporation whose only place of business is a hotel in Hong Kong. Robert Colan is a Vice President of Kidde Products, a Massachusetts corporation with its principal place of business in Massachusetts. Kidde distributes its products around the world, including Hong Kong. As a result, Kidde employees often visit Hong Kong. Five years ago, Colan went to Hong Kong and negotiated an agreement with Tak How whereby Kidde employees could stay at Tak How's hotel for a substantially reduced rate. This arrangement was confirmed in writing to Kidde corporate headquarters in Massachusetts. Following confirmation of this agreement, there were a number of telefax and telephone conversations between the Kidde headquarters and the hotel in Hong Kong. These calls and faxes involved employees securing room discounts at the hotel, as well as adjustments in the agreement setting out further discounts. Tak How had no other relationships in Massachusetts, except for the following. Tak How did send regular promotional announcements to its prior customers who lived in Massachusetts, many of whom happened to be Kidde employees. In addition, Tak How advertised in several world-wide business magazines. Tak How did not expect or intend for these advertisements to be viewed directly in Massachusetts, but the company made no effort to prevent any magazines in which it advertised from going there. Three years ago, after making a reservation by way of telefax from his Kidde office, Kidde vice-president Ralph Nowak and his wife Sally went to the Tak How Hotel in Hong Kong. Through the likely negligence of Tak How or one of its employees, Sally Nowak drowned in the swimming pool maintained by Tak How at the hotel.

Ralph Nowak has filed suit in Massachusetts against Tak How, which has appeared specially to contest personal jurisdiction. Massachusetts has a long arm statute that provides, in part: "A court of the Commonwealth may exercise jurisdiction on any basis consistent with the Constitutions of the Commonwealth and the United States."

Question

Are there enough "minimum contacts" or is there enough "purposeful availment" to justify personal jurisdiction over Tak How in Massachusetts? Why or Why not?

Longo v. O'Brien's Hotel Management Corporation

Frank Longo is a Nevada citizen. O'Brien's Hotel Management Corporation, is a corporate citizen of Idaho and operates hotels that contain gaming casinos in a number of Idaho locations. When Frank Longo tired of the gambling scene in Las Vegas and Lake Tahoe, he called one of O'Brien's Hotels/Casinos in Idaho, using O'Brien's toll free number listed in his Nevada telephone book, and made reservations for a week's stay. He was informed that his stay would cost $125 per night, plus tax, and he provided the hotel registration agent with his address and credit card number. When Longo and his wife arrived at O'Brien's and checked in, he confirmed that the room rate was $125 per night, plus tax. At the end of his week's stay, however, when he checked out of his room, Longo's bill included a charge of $5.00 per night as an "energy surcharge." The check-out clerk indicated that the hotel had to add this charge because of the high cost of fuel for heating and air conditioning. Following his return to Nevada, Longo, through his attorney, filed a class action lawsuit in Nevada state court on behalf of himself and "all other Nevada citizens similarly situated." In the complaint, Longo alleged that O'Brien's charged him and other guests an energy surcharge during their stays at hotels owned and operated by O'Brien's without providing notice of these charges during the reservation or check-in process. Longo further alleged that, in doing so, defendants charged more than the advertised or quoted price. These violations, it is alleged, constitute violations of Nevada's consumer protection statutes.

Questions

1. O'Brien's Hotel Management Corporation moved to dismiss the suit as soon as it was filed, alleging that O'Brien's has no offices, agents, or employees in Nevada and does not have any bank or other accounts there and that there was, therefore, no personal jurisdiction over the corporation. Assuming this information to be true, how should the Nevada court rule on the motion to dismiss? Why?

2. Assume that O'Brien's has a website. The O'Brien's website provides information about the hotels in Idaho, including virtual tours of the facilities, and provides room rates for single and group booking. It then provides O'Brien's toll free number for those interested. Assuming this information to be true, how should the Nevada court rule on the motion to dismiss for want of *specific* personal jurisdiction? Why?

3. Assume that O'Brien's website does more than provide information and give virtual tours of the facilities. On the website, potential customers can ask questions of the O'Brien's staff and book rooms through O'Brien's Reservations Direct. Assuming this information to be true, how should the Nevada court rule on the motion to dismiss for want of *specific* personal jurisdiction? Why?

Sawyer v. Woods, Poe, and Martin, PC

Ernest Sawyer, a citizen of West Virginia was killed when the aircraft he was flying, as a pilot under instruction, was struck over the West Virginia-Vermont border by an aircraft from Florida. Several months later, Ernest's mother and father, and only heirs, contacted a local attorney who referred them to the Chicago-based law firm of Woods, Poe, and Martin presumably because of that firm's reputation for expertise in aircraft litigation. After the Sawyers contacted Woods, Poe and Martin, an attorney for that firm sent a retainer agreement, which had already been executed on behalf of the firm, to the Sawyers in West Virginia. The retainer agreement included a provision granting the firm a lien upon any sum received in the plaintiffs' cause of action. The Sawyers signed the agreement and returned an executed original to the Chicago firm, which then transferred the case to its Washington, D.C. affiliate, which also operated under the Woods, Poe, and Martin name.

The case was assigned to Woods, Poe, and Martin attorney Michelle Wright. Wright is a Virginia resident. She was not licensed to practice law in West Virginia. Although Wright never personally met the plaintiffs, she sent at least fifteen letters to them in West Virginia and spoke to them by telephone on numerous occasions during the representation. Among the topics addressed in those communications was Wright's recommendation that Florida was the most advantageous forum for the wrongful death claim.

Michelle Wright affiliated with a Florida lawyer, and with the Florida lawyer, filed a wrongful death action in that state against the estate of the owner and operator of the other aircraft, a Florida citizen. Both lawyers signed the complaint as attorneys for the Sawyer family.

Following negotiations with the lawyer for the estate of the pilot of the other aircraft, Michelle Wright conveyed to the Sawyers a settlement offer of $155,000. While Mr. and Mrs. Sawyer were concerned thinking this amount to be too small, Michelle Wright wrote them a letter sent to their West Virginia home indicating her belief that it was in the Sawyers' best interest to settle the case. As a result of this advice, the Sawyers ultimately accepted the settlement offer.

The Sawyers were thus shocked to later learn that the estate of the flight instructor who was with Ernest Sawyer at the time of the accident settled with the estate of the Florida pilot for $500,000. That discovery prompted the Sawyers to file the present legal malpractice action against defendants in federal district court in West Virginia. They claim that Michell e Wright and the Woods, Poe, and Martin firm negligently negotiated an inadequate settlement of the wrongful death claim of their son's estate.

Question

Michelle Wright and her firm move to dismiss for lack of personal jurisdiction. How should the court rule? Why?

General versus Specific Jurisdiction

Reese v. Daniels

Eli Daniels is a citizen of West Virginia who is currently residing in college in Tennessee. To finance his college education, Daniels sells baseball cards over the internet at his website: "Cardsforall.com." Daniels advertises the cards and invites offers from "anyplace in the United States." Rebecca Reese is a citizen of Kentucky who is in the military and stationed in San Diego, California. Reese saw a rarely seen baseball card of her great-uncle by marriage, Pee Wee Reese on Daniels website and, after exchanging emails about price and shipping, Reese and Daniels agreed that Reese, who did not get much money as a GI stationed in California, would send $25 per month for the next 7 months to cover the cost of the card and shipping. Whenever he received payment from Rebecca, Daniels promptly sent her a receipt and a statement indicating the remaining balance on the account. In fact, Daniels did not really have the Reese card, just a picture of it, and, when he got Rebecca's final check, he sent Reese a substitute card of another New York shortstop, Phil Rizzuto. Daniels was happy to send this card to California, where Reese was stationed, because he had about ten other cards that he was shipping to California residents. In the same mailing, Daniels sent cards to five other states, including three cards to Kentucky, two cards each to four people with whom he did regular business in Louisiana, and one card each to Texas, Arizona and Florida. Rebecca Reese was, of course, infuriated to receive a Phil Rizzuto card when she wanted a Pee Wee Reese card and filed suit against Daniels. She was able to find Daniels at a baseball card show in New Mexico and served him with notice of the lawsuit there.

Questions

1. Assuming proper service of process, in which state(s) is there general personal jurisdiction for Reese's lawsuit against Daniels? Why is there general personal jurisdiction in the state(s) you selected?

2. Assuming proper service of process, in which state(s) is there specific personal jurisdiction for Reese's lawsuit against Daniels? Why is there specific personal jurisdiction in the state(s) you selected?

People's Petroleum, Inc. v. Strand, et als.

People's Petroleum is an Ohio Corporation largely, owned by James Korregan, an Ohio resident. Although its principal offices are located in Columbus, Ohio, People's Petroleum owns, leases, and operates various gas wells in Kentucky. Several years ago, People's Petroleum and Southern Gas Corporation, a Delaware corporation with its principal place of business in Kentucky agreed that Southern would sell to People's certain gas wells in Kentucky. Negotiations for this agreement took place at People's home office in Columbus, Ohio. The contract provided, among other things, as follows:

> Section 10.10. Governing Law. In any action relating to this agreement or the transactions contemplated hereby, this Agreement and the transactions contemplated hereby shall be construed in accordance with, and governed by, the laws of the State of Ohio.

Following the signing of this contract, People's Petroleum became the operator of the Kentucky wells previously run by Southern Gas, although the wells were operated in the name of Southern Gas, which continued as a Kentucky corporation.

Soon, however, People's Petroleum and Southern Gas had a falling out over numerous business issues. In fact, Southern Gas formed a new corporation, Strand Resources and, thereafter, both Southern Gas and Strand Resources competed with People's Petroleum in Kentucky.

As a result, People's Petroleum filed suit against Strand Resources, and Southern Gas Corporation alleging an illegal interference with the business relationships of People's Petroleum. The suit was filed in the United States District Court in Ohio.

Southern Gas Corporation moved to dismiss claiming a lack of personal jurisdiction. People's Petroleum argues that there is both general and specific jurisdiction.

Questions

1. Assuming that Ohio's Long Arm statute allows suits to the extent permitted by Due Process, is there specific personal jurisdiction over Southern Gas in the suit by People's Petroleum? Why or why not?

2 Assuming that Ohio's Long Arm statute allows suits to the extent permitted by Due Process, is there general personal jurisdiction in that same suit? Why or why not?

3. In answering either Question 1 or 2, would jurisdictional discovery be helpful? If so, what information would you seek?

Scott Lakin, as Receiver v. Alpine Savings

After a group of individuals engaged in an elaborate scheme that looted numerous insurance companies, over which the individuals had control, Scott Lakin was appointed by the court to serve as receiver for the now insolvent companies, all of which were corporate citizens of New Hampshire.

Alpine Savings is a federally-chartered savings bank with its principal place of business in the State of Georgia. In one of the fraudulent insurance schemes, the president of a New Hampshire insurance company opened a bank account at Alpine Savings in the insurance company's name and deposited some $69 million worth of premium payments into the account. The money was later transferred to another bank account and ultimately wound up in the former insurance company executive's Swiss bank account.

After discovery of this fraud, Scott Lakin, the Receiver, filed a complaint against Alpine Savings in the United States District Court for New Hampshire. The suit claimed that Alpine Savings was negligent and breached its contractual and fiduciary duties to its insurance company depositor when it permitted the $69 million to be released to the insurance executive without proper instruction from the company. Alpine Savings then filed a motion to dismiss for lack of personal jurisdiction, arguing that it has only one physical office located in New Hampshire, and that this office had nothing to do with the fraudulent insurance transaction. Alpine also indicated that it had virtually no contact with New Hampshire residents. Lakin countered that for three years prior to these events, Alpine Savings did have sufficient contacts with the State of New Hampshire. Lakin noted that Alpine Savings maintained home-equity loans and lines of credit to New Hampshire residents totaling around $10 million, or one percent of its loan portfolio. In addition, appellants noted that Alpine Savings maintained a Web site-www.Alpine.com/ banking on which Alpine Savings' services are offered to New Hampshire residents. In the alternative, receiver Lakin asked for jurisdictional discovery.

Questions

1. Can you make a case for specific personal jurisdiction over Alpine Savings in New Hampshire?

2. Can you make a case for general personal jurisdiction over Alpine Savings in New Hampshire?

3. If the court were to allow "jurisdictional discovery," what specifically should be asked? Why?

Transient Jurisdiction

Merchants Western Corp. v. Montgomery

Allan Montgomery, a citizen of California was employed in the Benicia, California plant of Merchants Western Corporation, a Wisconsin corporation. Merchants Western is a multifaceted corporation that deals generally in transportation. Several years ago, Merchants Western sent a letter to Montgomery outlining proposed terms for Merchants Western's sale of its Benicia Boom Truck Crane Dealership to Montgomery. Merchants Western believed the letter to be a non-binding general expression of intent, but Montgomery maintained that the letter was a binding and enforceable agreement.

Although the parties dispute many of the details surrounding events subsequent to the signing of this letter, the following three facts are undisputed. First, Montgomery came to Wisconsin with his attorney to meet with representatives of Merchants Western to discuss their disagreement over the letter. Second, on the day of this meeting, Merchants Western filed a lawsuit in Wisconsin state court seeking a declaration that it was not obligated to sell the Benicia property to Montgomery. Third, Merchants Western served Montgomery with process at the end of the meeting.

Montgomery now seeks to set aside the service of process and asked the circuit court to declare that it lacked jurisdiction over his person. The parties agree that, other than being in Wisconsin to discuss possible settlement of this dispute, Montgomery has no other contacts with the state.

Questions

1. How should the court rule on Montgomery's motion to quash service and dismiss the action? Why?

2. Suppose, instead, that Montgomery and his attorney had not scheduled a settlement discussion in Wisconsin. Instead, Montgomery's grandmother lives in the state. Posing as a friend of the grandmother, an employee of Merchants Western phoned Montgomery and told him that his grandmother had fallen terminally ill. Montgomery rushes from California and is met at the Milwaukee airport by a process server who gives him the Merchants Western suit. Does this change your answer? Why or why not?

Party Consent to Jurisdiction; Forum Selection/Choice of Law Clauses

Valley Vending v. SaveCo

Valley Vending conducted a business that owned and serviced novelty vending machines. It makes money placing these machines in various businesses. As a result, Valley Vending entered into an agreement with SaveCo that allowed Valley Vending to place machines in approximately 136 stores SaveCo operated in Minnesota, Nebraska, Iowa and Kansas. For its part, Valley Vending paid SaveCo a commission of approximately 40% of each machine sale. These terms were set out in a written contract. Some years after the contract began, SaveCo notified Valley Vending that SaveCo was terminating the parties' relationship. After receiving the notification, Valley Vending was contacted by Store Service, Inc, a vendor that would be replacing Valley at some of the SaveCo stores. Store Service inquired about purchasing equipment from Valley Vending that was in place in SaveCo stores where Store Service would be placing machines. Valley Vending sent a list of equipment for Store Service to consider. A dispute then arose among Valley Vending, Store Service and SaveCo. The dispute centered on statements made by some SaveCo managers that convinced Store Service that it would be too expensive for Store Service to purchase Valley Vending's equipment.

As a result of these statements, Valley Vending brought suit in state court in Minnesota. Valley Vending asserted SaveCo tortiously interfered with Valley Vending's business expectancy of selling Valley Vending's equipment to vendors that would be replacing it at SaveCo stores. Valley Vending contended it had a valid expectation that it could sell its vending machines in place to SaveCo approved vendors that would replace Valley Vending. SaveCo now moves to dismiss the Minnesota action based on paragraph 12 of the Valley Vending/SaveCo contract, which paragraph provided:

> SaveCo may terminate this Agreement at any time.
> Upon notice to [Valley Vending], either written or oral, all equipment belonging to [Valley Vending] shall be removed from SaveCo property within ten (10) days of receiving written notice. All costs of such removal shall be the responsibility of [Valley Vending]. In the event [Valley Vending] fails to remove its equipment SaveCo may use any reasonable means necessary to free the space and charge [Valley Vending] with all related costs. *In the event litigation arises between SaveCo and [Valley Vending] due to this Agreement, it is expressly agreed that such dispute will be governed by the laws of and tried in the State of Arkansas.* [Emphasis added.]

In its motion to dismiss, SaveCo makes two points:
> 1. Even if the court hears the matter, it must do so using Arkansas, not Minnesota, law
> 2. The court should dismiss the action because it is only properly filed in Arkansas.

Discuss both of these claims.

Jurisdiction to Determine Jurisdiction

Jackson Brothers, Inc. v. Baquet

MaryAnn Baquet is a citizen and resident of Utah and a University professor at a major public university in Utah. Sometime ago, MaryAnn purchased an item on-line from Jackson Brothers Women's Clothing, a Delaware corporation with its principal place of business in Georgia. When MaryAnn did not like the item she received, she told her credit card company that she had not made the purchase and the card company refused to honor the charge. Jackson Brothers has sued MaryAnn in state court in Georgia. When MaryAnn went to the Georgia court and filed a motion to dismiss for want of personal jurisdiction, the court authorized the parties to conduct limited discovery for the purposes of determining the personal jurisdiction issue. MaryAnn participated in discovery but continued to argue vigorously that personal jurisdiction did not exist in Georgia.

Question

Assume that the Georgia court found personal jurisdiction in Georgia and sets a trial date. Despite the lessons of *Pennoyer*, explain why MaryAnn cannot return to Utah, ignore the Georgia court, and challenge the personal jurisdiction issue if Jackson Brothers wins a judgment against her and tries to enforce that judgment in Utah.

Notice

City of Monroesville v. Locke

When Freddie Locke failed to pay the City of Monroesville's property taxes on the home in which Freddie was living, the City sued in state court to foreclose a tax lien on Freddie's house. In accordance with the applicable state service of process statute, the Monroesville Tax

Collector had the court clerk serve process on Freddie by publishing notice of the suit in the local newspaper for three consecutive weeks. Freddie Locke, in fact, saw this notice.

Question

Assume that Freddie does nothing and that the City obtains a default judgment against Freddie, can Freddie challenge the default on the basis that Monroesville did not serve him personally and therefore did not comply with the Constitutional requirements of *Mullane v. Central Hanover.?*

Eagen v. Zintner

Sara Belle Eagen, a citizen of Colorado, alleges that she was defrauded by Arthur Zintner, a citizen of Oregon, who, Sara Belle alleges, sold her real estate that was supposed to be "oceanfront" property. When Sara Belle finally saw the property, it was actually several miles from the shore. When she called Zintner about the problem, Zintner told Sara Belle to "wait until the earthquake. Then your property will be right on the ocean!" Sara Belle sued Zintner in the proper United States District Court. When the sheriff attempted to personally serve Zintner with notice of the lawsuit. Zintner, who had learned privately that the law suit had been filed, successfully avoided any contact with the sheriff. Because Zintner lived alone, the sheriff returned the suit papers to Sara Belle indicating that personal service over Zintner was not possible, even though Zintner's address was known. Acting pursuant to state statute, Sara Belle then "served" Zintner by sending a copy of the lawsuit to the address the sheriff knew to be Zintner's home and by publishing a copy of the lawsuit in a local newspaper for three straight weeks.

Question

Assume that Zintner did not answer, and that Sara Belle was granted a default judgment. Zintner now defends a proceeding compelling him to pay Sara Belle by arguing that he never received notice of the lawsuit. Who wins? Why?

Notice in International Cases

In re Bid Laden

A devastating truck bomb exploded outside an American embassy in Nairobi, Kenya. The blast killed more than 200 people, including 12 Americans, and wounded more than 4000 others. Most of the casualties were Kenyan. The families of three Kenyan victims, themselves citizens of Kenya sued Osama bin Laden and the organization known as al Qaeda for orchestrating the bombing. The suit was filed in the United States District Court for the District of Columbia. The suit sought compensatory damages and other relief. Shortly after filing the suit, the Kenyan plaintiffs moved to serve defendants bin Laden and al Qaeda by publication. The district court first found that no reasonable personal address could be found either for Bin Laden or al Qaeda and that neither had appointed an agent authorized to accept service of process. The court then granted the plaintiffs leave to serve those defendants by "publishing... notice for six weeks in the Daily Washington Law Reporter, the International Herald Tribune, and Al-Quds Al-Arabi (in Arabic)." The plaintiffs later advised the court that the notice had run in all three newspapers, as well as in two additional East African publications.

Questions

1. Did the plaintiffs' notice in this case satisfy the Federal Rules of Civil Procedure? Why or Why not?
2. Did the plaintiffs' notice satisfy *Mullane?* Why or Why not?

The Mechanics of Service

Khan v. Burton

When Doris Khan, Vincent Khan and Khan Imports, Inc., were named as defendants in a civil action instituted against them in the New Hampshire trial court by Second Community Bank, they hired Samuel V. Burton, Esq. ("Burton"), to represent them. Burton is a California attorney, who was known to the Khans from business dealings they had in California and who was admitted in New Hampshire for the limited purpose of trying the Second Community v. Khan et als suit in the state trial court. A substantial jury verdict was returned in favor of Second Community Bank.

Following that jury verdict, Doris Khan Vincent Khan and Khan Imports, Inc., filed suit against Samuel V. Burton in the United States District Court for the District of New Hampshire. That suit sought damages arising out of Burton's alleged legal malpractice in defending the Khans and Khan Imports in the prior action. That lawsuit was filed on November 1, two years ago.

The Khan's first attempted to effect service on Burton on or about November 11, two years ago. On that date, Khan's attorney wrote to Burton and requested that he waive service of summons. Burton did not respond to the request. Thereafter, on six occasions between March 9 and March 24, last year, a process server attempted unsuccessfully to effect personal service on Burton. On March 20, last year, the process server left a summons and copy of the Complaint at the Law Offices of Samuel V. Burton with "Kevin Hall, Esq.," who the process server identified as a "partner" of Burton. It is unclear if Hall was actually associated with Burton or merely shared office space with him.

On April 22, 1998, the Khan's attorney requested the entry of default pursuant to Rule 55(a). When the clerk entered default, the clerk also assessed costs of $150 for "refusal to waive service of process" on that date.

Questions

1. Was service effectively made?
2. What questions exist?

Long-Arm Jurisdiction

Longshore v. Stephens, et als.

Anthony Longshore, a citizen of North Carolina was married to Charlotte Longshore. That marriage ended in divorce, which was granted in North Carolina state court, and Charlotte Longshore moved back to Florida where her parents, Louise and Charles Norville were citizens. Charlotte Longshore became a citizen of Florida. Thereafter, Anthony Longshore paid maintenance of $310.00 per week to his wife, pursuant to the divorce decree that obligated him to make such payments unless or until Charlotte remarried. Several years after the divorce, Anthony learned that Charlotte had married Arnold Stephens shortly after the divorce had become final in North Carolina. Anthony Longshore then sued his ex-wife and her parents in state court in North Carolina alleging, in a tort action, that each of them agreed and conspired to defraud Anthony by using the U.S. mail in a scheme designed to conceal his ex-wife's remarriage so that Longshore would continue to make maintenance payments. Longshore's action sought to recover $40,500.00 in maintenance payments made after the remarriage plus pre-judgment interest and punitive damages. At the time of this suit, you may assume that the North Carolina Long Arm statute authorized suits against foreign defendants as a result of "the commission of a tortious act within this state."

1. Assume that the evidence will reveal that Charlotte Stephens continually asked Anthony to send her maintenance checks by mail to her parents home in Florida; that Anthony mailed 131 such checks to this address; that all of the checks were payable to "Charlotte Longshore;" that Charlotte picked up the checks from her parents, endorsed them as "Charlotte Longshore," and deposited them into a bank account in that name in Asheville, North Carolina; and that Anthony stopped sending the checks only after he learned via the Internet that his wife had remarried. Is there personal jurisdiction in North Carolina under the state's Long Arm statute? Why or why not?

2. If there is personal jurisdiction under the North Carolina Long Arm statute, is there personal jurisdiction over all defendants in North Carolina under the federal Constitution? Why or why not?

Suni v. Marner

Lisa Marner is a law student at the Hanover School of Law and is residing in Hanover, Missouri while attending school there. Lisa is, however, a citizen of Indiana. While driving home to Indiana, Lisa dozed off. As a direct result, Lisa's car collided with another car in which Mario Suni was a passenger. Mario was substantially injured in this collision, which took place in Illinois while Mario was on his way home to Kansas, where he is a citizen. For purposes of this problem, please assume that Kansas has a long arm statute that permits personal jurisdiction over "any person or entity causing tort damage to any Kansas citizen, regardless of where that damage takes place." For this problem, please assume that Kansas courts have found that tort damage, under the statute, takes place in the location of injury. Mario Suni has consulted a lawyer. That lawyer filed a suit against Lisa Marner on Mario's behalf in state court in Kansas.

Lisa Marner's lawyer moves to dismiss the case for want of personal jurisdiction in Kansas. Mario's lawyer points to the Kansas Long Arm statute for support. What result? Why?

Lamping v. Shuster

Dennis Lamping, a citizen of Illinois, entered into an oral contract with Marilyn Shuster, a California citizen to purchase four season tickets to the Chicago Cubs baseball team. When Shuster refused to go through with the sale, Lamping filed suit against Shuster in the state court in Illinois. For the purpose of this problem only, please assume that Illinois allows personal jurisdiction over persons who do either of the following:

    (1) The transaction of any business within this state;

    (2) The making of any contract within this state;

Despite this statute, Shuster moved to dismiss the state court action alleging an absence of personal jurisdiction. Uncontroverted affidavits agree that Shuster purchases Chicago Cubs season tickets annually through the mail and over the years, she has sold these season tickets to various individuals, including Lamping. Lamping makes contact with Shuster and sends her a check, from Illinois to California. Lamping does not allege that Shuster conducts any other business or maintains any other contacts within the state of Illinois. Shuster averred that she has not visited Illinois for ten years prior to this lawsuit.

Questions

    1. Can you make an argument that Lamping has either transacted business within the state of Illinois or has made a contract there?

    2. Assuming a court would find that Lamping had either transacted business within the state or made a contract there, is there personal jurisdiction over Lamping in Illinois? Why or why not?

The Limitations on Personal Jurisdiction Created by Venue Statutes Including Transfer of Venue

Robertson v. High Seas, Inc., et als.

On the high seas off the coast of Massachusetts, but not within Massachusetts territorial waters, Sarah Robertson, a cook on a merchant ship, and a citizen of New York, was injured due to the negligence of another. A fair estimate of Sarah's injuries would put them at approximately $125,000. On her behalf, Sarah Robertson's lawyer wants to file suit in federal court against the ship's owner, High Seas, Inc. a New York registered corporation whose corporate office are also in New York. The lawyer also wants to file suit against the manufacturer of the ship, Universal Ship Building, Inc., because of an allegation that the design of the ship may have been a part of the cause of Sarah's injuries. The manufacturer is a corporation incorporated in Delaware, with its corporate headquarters in Florida, but which does extensive business in Michigan, Washington state, Oregon, California and Virginia. Finally,

Sarah's attorney wants to file the suit against the ship's mate, Gerald Jones, who likely caused the accident. The mate's permanent home is New Jersey, but when the ship is not at sea, the mate lives in Maine. Regardless of the fact that the claim sounds in negligence, because the ship was at sea, the claim was filed as an Admiralty claim. Admiralty claims of this type are ones in which the federal court has exclusive jurisdiction.

Questions

1. Assuming there is one lawsuit, filed against the ship's owner, the ship's manufacturer, and the ship's mate, discuss all possible locations for venue.

2. Assume, instead that Sarah Robertson's lawyer has read about recent multimillion dollar verdicts in federal court in Oregon. As a result, Sarah's lawyer filed the action in the federal district court in Oregon closest to where the ship's manufacturer does most of its business in the state. The ship's manufacturer moved to dismiss the action from the federal court in Oregon for improper venue. What result? Why?

3. Assume the court does not dismiss for improper venue. What might the court do instead? How specifically should that be accomplished?

4. For this question only, assume that the ship's mate who likely caused this injury, Gerald Jones, is not a citizen of New Jersey, but is, instead, an alien. How does this change any of your answers to this problem? If Jones is an alien, could this lawsuit be brought in New Mexico?

Declining Personal Jurisdiction; Forum Non Conveniens

Howe v. Goldcorp

Reginald Howe, a citizen of Michigan, was a shareholder of Goldcorp, a Canadian Corporation. Howe claims that Goldcorp, its officers, its investment advisors, and its lawyers, all of whom are also Canadian citizens, violated United States securities statutes, primarily by failing to disclose adequately their intentions, plans, objectives and other circumstances related to their efforts to take over two other Canadian companies called Dickenson and Kam-Kotia. Goldcorp shares trade only on Canadian stock exchanges where anyone can buy them. Goldcorp sells its shares to residents of the United States only if they (or their agents) buy those shares in Canada. Goldcorp shares do not trade on stock exchanges (nor are they sold over the counter) in the United

States. In addition, Goldcorp sends annual reports, proxy statements and similar material to shareholders in whatever country they live. Thus, shareholders who live in the United States receive this material, sent as part of general, worldwide mailings. The same is true with dividend checks. All of the activities of Goldcorp, in Howe's claim, took place in Canada and were done by Canadian citizens. Howe has filed suit in federal court in Michigan and Goldcorp has accepted personal jurisdiction there.

Questions

Goldcorp has moved to dismiss the action under the doctrine of forum non conveniens. Please discuss the possibility of dismissal in light of each of the following:

1.   The fact that, under Canadian law, Howe cannot recover punitive damages in a Canadian court.
2.   The fact that Howe is an American citizen.
3   The fact that Canadian securities law is different from that in the United States.
4.   The fact that all of the witnesses and activities seem to have taken place in Canada.
5.   The fact that a court could find that either the public or private factors weigh in favor of dismissal.

Skews v. Chemical Enterprises, Inc.

Tammy Skews, a citizen of British Columbia, Canada, was employed as a painter by Edendale Restorations, a Vancouver, British Columbia company that performed restorative work on antique paintings. Generally, this work was done inside art museums and institutes. While working for Edendale at the Vancouver Art Institute, Tammy was seriously injured when a halogen lamp ignited vapors from a paint primer. A number of Tammy's coworkers and supervisors saw the accident take place. All of those workers are also citizens of British Columbia. The paint primer, however, was manufactured by Chemical Enterprises, Inc., a Florida corporation with its main office and factory in Ocala, in central Florida. Because she had almost $1 million in damages, Tammy Skews filed suit against Chemical Enterprises, Inc. in the United States District Court for the Central District of Florida based on diversity of citizenship. Chemical Enterprises, Inc. moves to dismiss the case based on forum non conveniens.

Questions

1. Based on these facts, does venue appear correct in the United States District Court for the Central District of Florida? Why or why not? What statutes are involved?

2. Why is a motion to dismiss used here? Why not a motion to transfer?

3. Assuming venue is proper, what factors should the court consider in determining the motion to dismiss based on forum non conveniens?

CHAPTER 2

SUBJECT MATTER JURISDICTION AND REMOVAL

Federal Question

Bingham v. James

Caleb Bingham, a citizen of Oklahoma, believed that he was the owner of a certain parcel of land just outside Stillwater, Oklahoma. The land had been used primarily for farming and Caleb had an overseer who watched over various sharecropping tenants on the property. Caleb was thus surprised one day when he received a call from his overseer indicating that Thomas James and his wife, both of whom were citizens of Oklahoma, were on the property and claimed ownership of it. James and his wife had brought in portable buildings and were engaged in construction on the land in what looked like an attempt to set up residence on the building. Caleb immediately called his lawyer and wanted to begin an action to have the James family evicted from the property. When Caleb's lawyer searched the land title to the property, the lawyer found some interesting history. As a result, the complaint that the lawyer filed on behalf of Caleb Bingham against Thomas and Harriet James stated as follows:

1. Caleb Bingham is the owner in fee and entitled to the immediate possession of the property;

2. Thomas and Harriet James had forcibly taken possession and were wrongfully keeping Caleb Bingham out of possession of a portion of the property;

3. That as a direct result, Caleb Bingham was damaged by the loss of the use of a portion of his land;

4. That Thomas and Harriet James claimed ownership of the land as a result of a certain deed to them by Robert Morris, now deceased;

5. That Robert Morris had purportedly received a deed from the Choctaw and Chickasaw Indian nations;

6. That any such deed to Robert Morris was void under an act of the United States Congress restricting the alienation of lands previously granted to the Choctaw and Chickasaw Indian nations.

7. That as a direct result, any claim to ownership by Thomas and Harriet James was void and of no effect.

8. That as a direct result, Thomas and Harriet James should be evicted from Caleb Bingham's land and should be required to pay damages for their impermissible use of the land.

This lawsuit was filed by Bingham's lawyer in the United States District Court for the Eastern District of Oklahoma. James' lawyer filed an immediate motion to dismiss for want of federal court subject matter jurisdiction.

Questions

1. Does the action by Bingham against James implicate federal law?

2. Does the action involve a federal question?

3. If they are different, how do you explain any differences between your answers to questions 1 and 2?

Lamberg v. Living Dreams, Inc.

Stuart L. Lamberg is a Nevada attorney and citizen who maintains an estate planning practice in Las Vegas, Nevada. Living Dreams, Inc. is a Nevada corporation that placed an advertisement in a Reno newspaper, offering living trust seminars and estate planning services. As a corporation, Living Dreams, Inc. is not authorized to practice law. In fact, depending on exactly what is stated in their seminars, you should assume for the sake of this problem only that the Nevada Supreme Court, which exercises control over the practice of law, has determined that general estate planning services are the practice of law because knowledge of the law is essential to the offering of such services.

When Mr. Lamberg saw the ads for Living Dreams, Inc., he brought an action in the federal district court for the District of Nevada against Living Dreams, Inc, seeking to enjoin them from "ongoing acts of illegal advertising" and from future violations of Nevada law prohibiting the unauthorized practice of law.

In the complaint, Mr. Lamberg alleged, among other things:

1. Living Dreams, Inc., produces estate planning seminars and services;

2. Such conduct constitutes the "practice of law" under Nevada law;

3. Living Dreams, Inc. is not an attorney and, in fact, no attorney admitted to the practice of law in Nevada is the president, an officer or director of Living Dreams, Inc;

4. The conduct by Living Dreams, Inc. is not protected commercial speech under the First Amendment of the United States Constitution;

5. The conduct by Living Dreams, Inc. does not enjoy any "associational freedom" protected by the First Amendment of the United States Constitution;

6. Because the conduct by Living Dreams, Inc. is not protected by the First Amendment of the United States Constitution, because the conduct is the practice of law under Nevada law, and because Living Dreams is not an attorney, the conduct constitutes the unauthorized practice of law;

7. As a result, this conduct should be enjoined.

Upon receipt of this complaint, the attorney for Living Dreams, Inc. immediately moves to dismiss for want of a federal question.

Questions

1. Does the action by Lamberg against Living Dreams implicate federal law?

2. Does the action involve a federal question?

3. If they are different, how do you explain any differences

between your answers to questions 1 and 2

Grable & Sons Metal Products, Inc v. Darue Engineering & Manufacturing

Some time ago, the Internal Revenue Service seized Michigan real property belonging to Grable & Sons Metal Products, Inc., a corporate citizen of Michigan, to satisfy Grable's federal tax delinquency. Under federal statute, the IRS was required to provide notice of this seizure to Grable and Sons and there is no dispute that Grable received actual notice by certified mail before the IRS sold the property to satisfy the debt. At a tax sale, the IRS sold the property to Darue Engineering & Manufacturing, another Michigan corporate citizen. Grable received notice of this sale and, when Grable did not exercise its right under federal statute to pay the back due taxes and reclaim the land, the IRS issued a quitclaim deed to Darue Engineering.

Five years later, Grable & Sons Metal Products, Inc brought an action in the federal court in Michigan against Darue Engineering and Manufacturing. That action sought to quiet title to the affected property in Grable & Sons. Part of the action read as follows:

1. Grable & Sons Metal Products, Inc. was the owner of a certain piece of real estate located in the State of Michigan;

2. The Internal Revenue Service seized said property, purportedly to satisfy delinquent federal taxes owed by Garble & Sons;

3. The IRS then sold the property, alleging that it conveyed title to Darue Engineering and Manufacturing;

4. Notice of the seizure, notice of the sale and notice of the right to redeem this property, all required by federal law, were not provided to Grable & Sons Metal Products, Inc;

5. As a direct result, any title purportedly conveyed to Darue Engineering and Manufacturing is void and of no effect;

6. As a direct result, title to said property should be exclusively vested in Grable and Sons Metal Products, Inc.

Upon the filing of this suit, the attorney for Darue Engineering immediately moves to dismiss the case for want of a federal question, arguing that this is no more than a quiet title action.

Questions

1. Does the action by Grable & Sons against Darue Engineering implicate federal law?

2. Does the action involve a federal question?

3. If they are different, how do you explain any differences between your answers to questions 1 and 2?

Dean, et al. v. E.B. Wireless

According to experts in these matters, wireless cellular telephones emit a low level of radio frequency radiation, a form of electromagnetic energy, from their antennae when they communicate with the base stations needed to allow telephone service coverage. While it is well established that exposure to high levels of RF radiation can cause adverse health effects, there is no scientific consensus on the effects of low level exposure. The Federal Communications Commission (FCC) requires all transmitters that emit RF radiation to be authorized by the agency before they are marketed or sold. Pursuant to the National Environmental Policy Act of 1969, which requires agencies to consider the impact of their actions on the quality of the human environment, the FCC has promulgated rules that limit the amount of RF radiation that FCC-regulated transmitters, including wireless telephones, may emit.

Based on this scientific data, Aaron Dean, Sharon Anderson, LaVelle Harrington, and Marshall Roberts, all citizens of Idaho, have filed suit in the federal court in Idaho, against E.B. Wireless, a corporate citizen of Idaho. E.B. manufactures, under several brand names, wireless cellular phones. The claim by Dean, Anderson, Harrington and Roberts is that (1) wireless telephones manufactured by E.B. Wireless emit an unsafe level of RF radiation and (2) E.B. Wireless, in knowing this, negligently and fraudulently endangered the consuming public by marketing wireless telephones without headsets. Dean, Anderson, Harrington and Roberts all claim that they were exposed to the risk of adverse biological effects from the RF radiation emitted by their wireless telephones when they used the telephones without headsets. Damages are sought for the violations.

Attorneys for E.B. Wireless have filed a motion to dismiss the action in federal court for want of a federal question.

Question

What result on this motion? Why?

Diversity

Generally

Richards v. Elvin

Enid Elvin, a citizen of Nebraska, abandoned her home in

Nebraska and began to roam from place to place around the world. Elvin never intended to make any place h er home or to stay anywhere indefinitely or permanently. While she was living in Laramie, Wyoming, Elvin was sued by Archibald Richards, a citizen of Wyoming, in the United States District Court for Nebraska on a state breach of contract claim for $100,000, arising out of property Elvin had previously promised to sell to Richards.

Question

Is there federal diversity over this claim? Why or why not?

When is Diversity Necessary?

Kathy v. Dawkins and Babcock

Roberta Kathy, a citizen of North Carolina, was visiting her friend Caroline Dawkins in Dallas, Texas. Caroline is a citizen of Texas. Also visiting was another friend of Caroline's, Charles Babcock, who is a citizen of Oregon. While swimming in Caroline's Dallas swimming pool, Charles pushed Kathy to the bottom of the pool. Unbeknownst to either of them, the pool had a very shallow, and unmarked bottom. As a result of being pushed to the bottom, Kathy broke her nose and jaw. Kathy, who was a model, was thereafter forced to miss several modeling jobs in her home state of North Carolina. Because of that, Kathy has contemplated moving to Houston, where she believes she will be better able to recover from her injuries. A fair estimate is that Kathy has $185,000 worth of provable damages. Assume that Kathy's lawyer files suit against both Caroline, for not telling her about the depth of the pool, and Charles, for pushing her to the bottom. The suit is filed in federal court and alleges diversity of jurisdiction. Shortly after her lawyer files suit, Roberta Kathy did move to Houston, Texas, to pursue some modeling opportunities. When she arrived in Texas, Kathy changed her voting address and obtained a new drivers' license in Texas. She anticipates spending the balance of her career there.

Questions

1. The attorney for Caroline Dawkins seeks to dismiss the action alleging an absence of diversity, claiming that Roberta Kathy's move to Houston has eliminated federal jurisdiction. What result? Why?

2. Assume that Roberta Kathy completed her move, changed her voting address and obtained a new drivers' license in Texas the day before the complaint was filed in the case. Would that change your answer? How? Why?

3. Assume that Charles Babcock was a citizen of Texas, not a citizen of Oregon. Would this change your answer? How? Why?

Diversity and Marriage

Alberts v. Banks

Zach Alberts, a citizen of Wisconsin, attends school in South Dakota and comes home during college breaks. Zach is married to Rachael, a citizen of South Dakota and, while in college, they live in college housing at the University of South Dakota. Zach contemplates remaining in South Dakota after graduation to teach, but has not yet fully decided. At a pep rally for the South Dakota football team, Zach is struck by a mascot representing rival South Dakota State University. The South Dakota State mascot was being worn by Allison Banks, a citizen of South Dakota. Zach was incensed at being struck by the SDSU mascot. While Zach did have a sore neck and did seek some assistance from a chiropractor, he did not go to the hospital and had no other medical bills. Nonetheless, Zach filed suit against Allison in the United States District Court for the District of South Dakota alleging personal injuries in excess of $75,000.

Questions

1. Allison Bank's lawyer moves to dismiss claiming that Zach is a citizen of South Dakota and, as a result, there is no diversity. What result? Why?

2. Allison Bank's lawyer moves to dismiss for want of the correct amount in controversy, alleging that Zach's injuries are not likely to total $75,000. What test will the court use to resolve this motion?

Diversity and Corporations

Cardinal Corp., et als v. Capricorn Corp., et als

The Cardinal Corporation, which is incorporated in Delaware with its principal place of business in Texas, and Royal Corporation, which is incorporated in Delaware with its principal place of business in California, sued Capricorn Corporation, which is incorporated in Michigan with its principal place of business in Pennsylvania, and Dweeble Corporation, which is incorporated in Pennsylvania with its principal place of business in New Jersey. The case was filed in a United

States District Court in Pennsylvania on a state breach of contract claim for $6,000,000.

Questions

1. Why is diversity proper under these facts?
2. Suppose the action were filed in a United States District Court in Montana. Is diversity still proper? Why or why not?

Pleading Diversity

In re Judge Stephanie Smith's Law Clerk

As law clerk for Judge Stephanie Smith of the United States District Court in your state, you have been asked to review the jurisdictional allegations of the following federal diversity complaints. Judge Smith is known to be very precise in requiring a "proper" basis for federal jurisdiction. Which of these jurisdictional allegations should Judge Smith approve?

1. Plaintiff is a resident of the State of Minnesota. Defendant's citizenship is unknown to the Plaintiff. The amount in controversy, exclusive of interest and costs, exceeds the sum of $75,000.
2. Plaintiff is a domiciliary of the State of Missouri and defendant is domiciled in the State of Minnesota. The amount in controversy, exclusive of interest and costs, exceeds the sum of $75,000.
3. Plaintiff is a citizen of the State of Missouri and defendant is a citizen of the State of Minnesota. The amount in controversy, exclusive of interest and costs, exceeds the sum of $75,000.

Diversity and Aliens

Alberts v. McAmbridge

Nora Alberts is a citizen of Colorado. While driving on Interstate Highway 70 in Illinois, Nora was involved in an automobile accident with Stephen McAmbridge. McAmbridge is a citizen of Ireland who is living and working in Pueblo, Colorado and admitted as a resident alien there. McAmbridge believes the accident was Alberts' fault and Alberts believes the accident was McAmbridge's fault. Alberts sues in the federal court in Illinois alleging the negligence of McAmbridge. Alberts claims injuries totaling approximately $150,000.

Question

Assume that McAmbridge moves to dismiss Albert's claim for failure to state a claim. While the court denies both of this motion, the court does dismiss the matter on its own motion? Why? What right does the court have to do this?

Cartier v. Davis

Miquel Cartier, a citizen of Argentina admitted to permanent residence in the United States and domiciled in California, sues Torrence Davis, a citizen of Texas, for $100,000 on a breach of contract claim arising under the law of Argentina in a United States District Court in Texas.

Question

Does the United States District Court, in Texas have subject matter jurisdiction over this lawsuit? Why or why not?

Diversity and Partnerships

Lennex, Corporation v. DataDoo Partnership

DataDoo is a partnership that has developed a computer program that cleans and reconditions computers at the close of a day's business. The DataDoo program eliminates downloaded data that otherwise clogs a computer and makes the computer run slower. DataDoo, the partnership, and DataDoo, the program, are the brainchild of its partners, all of whom met in college in southern California. Albert Goings, one of the partners, is a citizen of California; Brenda Santoro, another of the partners, is a citizen of Oregon. The final two partners, Manual Delepiere and Benita Bonella are both citizens of Mexico, living in southern California, but who are not admitted to permanent residence in the United States.

One of DataDoo's first customers was Lenex Corporation, a corporate citizen of Mexico, that made drive systems for one of the world's largest computer manufacturers. By contract, DataDoo supplied the DataDoo system to Lenex, which incorporated it into their drive system, until something horrible happened. The DataDoo system itself was infected with a virus that seriously incap acitated any system operating with the Lenex drivers.

As a result of these events, Lenex Corporation filed suit in the proper United States District Court in California against DataDoo

Partnership. After the pleadings were finalized and during discovery, both Manual Delepiere and Benita Bonella were granted permanent resident status in the United States and they continue to live in California. As discovery nears completion, the attorney for DataDoo files suggestions with the court arguing that the court is without subject matter jurisdiction.

Questions

1. Having answered and participated in discovery, how can DataDoo seek dismissal now?
2. What result on this motion? Why?
4. What is the impact of the fact that Delepiere and Bonella became permanent resident aliens during the course of the suit?

Amount in Controversy

Generally

Delfino v. Gaudette

Audrey Delfino is a citizen of Alabama living in Arizona. Audrey sues Rudolph Gaudette, a physician and citizen of Florida, on a breach of implied consent claim arising when Gaudette did not properly advise Delfino of the risks of surgery that Dr. Gaudette was going to perform on Delfino. The suit is for $60,000 and is filed in a United States District Court in Texas, where Dr. Gaudette resides during the winter and where he can be served. In a second count, Delfino alleges that Dr. Gaudette has committed medical malpractice because of the failure to give Delfino proper advice of the risks of this surgery. This claim is for $70,000.

Question

Dr. Gaudette's lawyer moves to dismiss claiming there is an insufficient amount in controversy for diversity jurisdiction. Delfino's lawyer argues that the two separate claims, filed in two separate counts can be aggregated for diversity purposes. Who is right? Why? Should the suit be dismissed? Why or why not?

Amount in Controversy and Class Actions

In re Lakeshore Resort & Yacht Club Class Action

Several years ago, Sundown Estates Development Company began construction of a hotel and twenty-unit condominium resort on a tract of land located on the shores of Lake Ferguson in Stillwater, Arkansas. Sundown Estates owned the hotel and resort property for a few years until it conveyed the resort property to the Lakeshore Resort & Yacht Club. Sundown Estates continued to construct a hotel on the tract of land surrounding the resort property.

Thereafter, Lakeshore started a time-share project organized pursuant to the provisions of the Arkansas Time-Share Act. Contemporaneous with its organization of the time-share project, Lakeshore LP reached a license agreement with Sundown Estates that allowed individual purchasers of Lakeshore's time-share units to use hotel parking, as well as the recreational amenities contemplated in the operation of the hotel. As a result, Lakeshore's master deed for all of its time-share owners reflected this agreement. Following registration of its time-share Master Deed with the state, Lakeshore began marketing time-share interests to individuals. Among those who purchased time-shares were Albert and Mary Jenkins; Leroy and Doris Kessler; Harold and Annie Carpenter; and Ruben and Harriet Blaze. Each of these purchasers received a Warranty Deed that incorporated by reference the Lakeshore Resort Master Deed and gave the purchasers a time-share interest in the resort for twenty years. For each family mentioned in this problem, their time share interest was two weeks out of the calendar year, and the Warranty Deed named the two specific weeks. Additionally, a sales brochure given to the purchasers represented that "[a]s a Lakeshore owner all of the facilities at the [Hotel] are yours to use and enjoy."

The hotel honored the terms of the license agreement for awhile. Problems arose, however, both financial and otherwise and after several changes in management, the hotel refused to allow Lakeshore time-share holders to use hotel facilities, claiming that Lakeshore had breached its agreement with hotel. The Lakeshore time-share units have been unusable ever since.

Because their time-share units are essentially unusable, Albert and Mary Jenkins; Leroy and Doris Kessler; Harold and Annie Carpenter; and Ruben and Harriet Blaze have filed suit, along with about 70 other time-share owner couples, in federal court against Lakeside alleging breach of their Warranty Deed. You may assume that roughly half of the plaintiffs are citizens of a state different from Lakeside, which is an Arkansas corporation. The balance of the plaintiffs are all citizens of Arkansas.

Question

At a motion hearing last week on this matter, the trial judge inquired of the parties: "How is there diversity jurisdiction in this case?" First, nearly half of the plaintiffs are citizens of the defendant's state. Second, while it is clear to me that the total damages of all the plaintiffs probably exceeds $5,000,000, I do not see how any individual plaintiff's damages could ever exceed $75,000." Discuss.

Amount in Controversy and Non-Damage Actions

Bishop v. Townhouse, Corporation

Alfred Bishop, a citizen of Texas, is the owner of a small tract of land in downtown Austin, Texas. The total value of Bishop's land is less than $50,000. Adjoining Bishop's land is the 20 story office building of Townhouse Corporation. Townhouse's office building has a value of approximately $80 million. During a recent survey of his land, Bishop discovered that the Townhouse Corporation office building encroached approximately 1.789 inches onto his land.

Bishop has contacted a lawyer and wants to sue Townhouse Corporation to have the office building removed because of its encroachment onto his land. Townhouse is incorporated in Delaware and has its main office in Chicago. Townhouse, however, only has one asset, the office building in Austin. With the exception of a secretary who works in the small office in Chicago, all other Townhouse employees are at the Austin office building.

Questions

1. On these facts, can Bishop sue Townhouse Corporation in the federal district court in Delaware? Why or why not?

2. Assume that, under the facts, Townhouse, Corporation has a substantial business presence in Chicago and that its principal corporate offices are located there. As a result, Bishop can sue Townhouse in a proper federal district court based on diversity jurisdiction. Bishop's suit seeks to compel Townhouse to remove the encroaching building. Townhouse moves to dismiss alleging an insufficient amount in controversy to justify federal diversity jurisdiction. How should the court rule on this motion? Why?

Supplemental Jurisdiction

Robbins v. Sparkling Soda, Inc.

When nine-year-old Jennifer Robbins, a citizen of New Hampshire, popped the top off a can of Sparkling Soda, Inc.'s "Sparkleberry Strawberry" soda, a defect in the can and its top caused a large gash in Jennifer's hand. The injury went deep into Jennifer's finger, cutting tendons and arteries. Jennifer suffers the prospect of permanent injury to her hand as a result of this incident. A reasonable jury could calculate her injuries at about $500,000. Jennifer filed suit in the United States District Court against Sparkling Soda, Inc., a corporate citizen of Delaware alleging both a design defect in the can and negligence in failing to warn consumers about the dangers of the pop-tops. Additional plaintiffs also joined the lawsuit. Jennifer's father, who was responsible for Jennifer's hospital and medical bills, claimed that he had suffered damage because of those bills in the amount of $60,000. Jennifer's mother, who was with Jennifer at the time of the incident, claimed that she suffered from severe emotional distress as a direct result of the actions and that she had received psychiatric treatment for her injuries in the amount of $50,000.

Question

Sparkling Soda, Inc. moved to dismiss the claims by Jennifer's father and mother, because these claims did not meet the jurisdictional amount in controversy. The lawyers for both Jennifer's father and mother claimed that these claims should be permitted pursuant to the federal district court's Supplemental Jurisdiction. What result? Why?

Tenneco v. Cumberland Bank

Tenneco is a Tennessee corporation engaged in the manufacture of airline parts. The Cumberland Bank is a corporate citizen of Alabama that offers regional banking operations in states throughout the south. In Tennessee, Cumberland operates through Cumberland Valley Trust, a wholly owned subsidiary and another Alabama corporation. In an action based on diversity of citizenship filed in a proper federal district court against Cumberland Bank, Tenneco alleged that Susan Owen, a former employee of Cumberland Valley Trust forged the signature of Cumberland Valley Trust's chief executive, William Best, on payroll checks belonging to Tenneco. Both Owen and Best are citizens of Tennessee. Tenneco claims that Owen was acting without authorization and with the intent to steal from Tenneco. Tenneco further alleges in its Complaint that Cumberland Valley Trust knew or should have known that the signatures affixed to the corporate checks in question by Owen were "obvious forgeries," and should not have honored these checks. The amount alleged to have been stolen exceeds $200,000 and Tenneco seeks that amount from Cumberland alleging the negligence of Cumberland in honoring these obvious forgeries. Some time after the case was filed, Tenneco sought to amend adding William Best as a plaintiff. William Best, it is alleged, is a guarantor for the debts of Tenneco and claims to have suffered damage as a result of the actions of Cumberland Bank in honoring these fraudulent checks. Although the motion to amend was made by Tenneco, it is not asserting any direct claim against Best at this time. Best, if added, will, however, assert a claim against Cumberland. That claim, while somewhat uncertain, almost certainly will be in the range of $35,000.

Questions

1. If William Best independently sued Cumberland Valley, on these facts, would that suit properly be in the federal court?
2. Is there supplemental jurisdiction over Best's claim against Cumberland Valley? Why or why not.

Noah's Ark Insurance Co. v. Business Reinsurance, Inc., et als

Noah's Ark Insurance Company is a Delaware corporation which writes multi-line insurance for both business and personal clients in most of the states in the country. Following a series of environmental disasters, all taking place in the State of Minnesota, Noah's Ark paid claims for pollution losses on three separate insurance policies written to Braun Petroleum, Denton Industrial Waste Corporation, and Molten Metals, Inc. Noah's Ark had purchased separate reinsurance policies to cover potential environmental losses for these three industrial clients. As a result of the loss paid on behalf of Braun Petroleum, Noah's Ark made claim for prorated reinsurance benefits of $60,000 to Equitable Reinsurance, Inc., a California corporation. As a result of the loss paid on behalf of Denton Industrial Waste Corporation, Noah's Ark made a claim for prorated reinsurance benefits of $50,000 to American Reinsurance, Inc., another California corporation, and, as a result of the loss paid on behalf of Molten Metals, Inc., Noah's Ark has made a claim for prorated reinsurance benefits of $125,000 to Business Reinsurance, Inc., also a California corporation. When none of the reinsurance companies responded to Noah's Ark's demand for coverage, Noah's Ark filed a diversity suit in an appropriate United States district court against Business Reinsurance, Inc. seeking reinsurance coverage of $125,000 on the Molten Metals loss. Prior to answer by Business Reinsurance, Noah's Ark amended its complaint to assert two additional claims; one for $60,000 against Equitable Reinsurance on the Braun claim and one for $50,000 against American Reinsurance on the Denton Industrial Waste claim.

Question

All three of the defendants, Business Reinsurance, Equitable Reinsurance and American Reinsurance move to dismiss Noah's Ark's complaint on the basis that there is no federal jurisdiction. What result? Why?

Removal and the Process of Removal

Jones v. Daymare Christian School

The Daymare Christian School, Inc., is a private Christian elementary school, and is a corporate citizen of Kansas. It requires that its teachers subscribe to a particular set of religious beliefs, including belief in the internal resolution of disputes through the "Biblical chain of command." As a contractual condition of employment, teachers must agree to present any grievance to their immediate supervisor and to acquiesce in the final authority of the corporation's board of directors, rather than to pursue a remedy in civil court. Mabel Jones, a citizen of Kansas, is a teacher in the Daymare Christian School. When Mabel Jones became pregnant, she was advised that her employment contract would not be renewed because of Daymare's religious doctrine and rule that mothers should stay home with their preschool age children. When Jones sought help from an attorney, Daymare then terminated her because Jones refused to abide by the school's dispute resolution doctrine. The teacher then filed suit in state court alleging that Daymare's decision constituted unlawful sex discrimination in violation of state law, and you may assume that such a state law exists.

Daymare countered with an answer that asserted that the federal Constitution's First Amendment prevented the state court from favorably considering Jones' suit. Upon the filing of this answer, Daymare sought to remove the case to the federal district court for the District of Kansas. Mabel Jones opposed this motion.

Questions

1. Is the action by Jones against Daymare School, and Daymare's defense, an action that implicates federal law?

2. Is the action one that Daymare can remove to federal court?

3. If they are different, how do you explain any differences between your answers to questions 1 and 2?

4. Who should control whether a case is set in federal or state court? Why? Why is it important to respect that choice?

Snell v. Baker Corporation

Loretta Snell, a citizen of Iowa, sues Baker Corporation, a Nebraska corporation whose principal place of business is in Nebraska, and Shane Morton, a citizen of Illinois, in state court in Illinois as a result of an alleged contract breach involving computer parts manufactured by Baker and sold by Morton to Snell. The suit seeks damages against both defendants jointly in the amount of $300,000. Baker Corporation seeks to remove the case to the federal district court. Snell resists.

Question

The court denies the petition for removal. Why?

Process of Removal

Shelter Insurance Co. v. Sludge, Inc.

Shelter Insurance, a corporation which is incorporated in and has its principal place of business in Missouri, contracts with Sludge, Inc. to insure Sludge against tort liability arising out of Sludge's incineration business. Sludge is incorporated in Missouri, but has its principal place of business in Reno, Nevada. After Sludge is accused of violating federal environmental laws, Shelter sues Sludge in state court asking the court to declare that Shelter is not liable under the policy for any tort claims asserted against Sludge for violating federal environmental statutes. Shelter claims that there is a federal statute specifically forbidding insurance reimbursement. After the case is filed in state court, Sludge seeks to remove the case to the proper United States District Court. Shelter opposes removal.

Questions

1. What specifically, will Sludge say in its removal petition?

2. Where will the removal petition be filed? When must it be filed? Who decides if the case is removed? Can the court from which the case is being removed prevent removal? Why or why not?

3. Will removal be successful? Why or why not?

4. What happens if the federal court eventually decides that the case should not have been removed or that state claims are actually more important to the outcome then federal claims?

NCAA v. Ballentine Brewing Co.

Ballentine Brewing Co, Inc., is a corporate citizen of Maryland which has always advertised heavily in televised sporting events, especially baseball. During the commercial build up to the most recent National Collegiate Athletic Association's annual men's baseball world series, Ballentine ran a series of advertisements offering tickets to the college world series in Omaha, Nebraska to those who could be the first to answer a series of trivia questions about NCAA baseball. Ballentine offered 20 sets of tickets to various games, worth an aggregate amount of approximately $2,000. In addition, each winner received overnight accommodations in Omaha, the total of which was worth approximately $5,000.

The problem with this advertising was that Ballentine was not a commercial partner of the NCAA, and did not have permission to use either the NCAA's name or images of any of the NCAA's commercial "properties," such as the college World Series. As a result, the NCAA, a citizen of Indiana, sued Ballentine Brewing Co., Inc. in state trial court in Nebraska, the home of the College World Series, about which the Ballentine promotion is about. Ballentine has advertised this promotion and has several wholesale distributors in Nebraska and can thus be "found" there. The suit seeks both money damages and injunctive relief to prevent Ballentine from continuing the promotion.   Ballentine has filed the necessary petition to have the case removed to the United States District Court for the District of Indiana.

Questions

1. What documents does Ballentine need to file to accomplish removal?

2. Where are these documents filed?

3. If the NCAA wants to oppose the removal of the case, alleging that there is an insufficient amount in controversy to justify removal, how does it go about doing that? What documents does it need to file? Where?

4. If the NCAA does challenge diversity based on the amount in controversy, who must prove there is enough in dispute?

CHAPTER 3

ABSTENTION AND ANTI-INJUNCTION ACT

Anti-Injunction Act

In re Building Materials, Inc. Class Action

Building Materials, Inc. manufactures building materials from industrial wood products and wood pulp. One of its products was "Inner-Seal Siding," an exterior composite-wood siding designed to resemble conventional lumber for use on residential and other structures. Building Materials provided a 25-year limited warranty with the purchase of Inner-Seal Sid ing. Additionally, Building Materials registered "Inner-Seal Siding," as a registered trademark.

Approximately 10 years ago, owners of structures on which Inner-Seal Siding had been installed brought a class action lawsuit in the District Court for the District of Oregon for damages resulting from the failure of Inner-Seal Siding. The class plaintiffs alleged that the siding had prematurely rotted, buckled, cracked and otherwise deteriorated when exposed to normal weather conditions and was not nearly as durable as regular wood or other commercially available siding.

The federal action, which covered a nationwide class of claimants, settled shortly after it was filed. The settlement was binding on all class members, save those who timely requested exclusion from the class. All members of the "Settlement Class" were "barred and permanently enjoined from prosecuting 'Settled Claims' ... against Building Materials." The "Settlement Class" was defined as "all persons who have owned, own, or subsequently acquire property on which Inner-Seal Siding has been installed prior to January 1, nine years ago." The settlement did not cover claims arising from the failure of new siding installed after January 1, nine years ago. The settlement agreement excluded claimants who timely requested exclusion from the class and claimants who were members of a preexisting certified class action then in existence in Florida.

In addition to the release of claims against Building Materials, the class members released all claims related to the failure of InnerSeal Siding (installed prior to January 1, nine years ago) against persons or entities "involved in the distribution, installation, construction and first time sale of structures with Inner-Seal Siding." This provision was included to foreclose the possibility that class members would bring claims against businesses located in the Inner-Seal Siding chain of distribution. Claims against Building Materials by persons or entities within the chain of distribution were not released. The district court retained "[E]xclusive and continuing jurisdiction over the Actions and Parties, including all members of the Class, the administration and enforcement of the settlement, and the benefits to the Class." This included supervision, implementation, enforcement and interpretation of the settlement.

Lester, Inc. is a New Mexico corporation that designs, constructs and sells pre-engineered wood buildings for livestock confinement. Lester purchased Inner-Seal Siding from Building Materials, Inc. during the period covered by the settlement and incorporated the siding into the structural wall panels of buildings sold to its customers. As a distributor of buildings equipped with Inner-Seal Siding, Lester was not a class member and was not a party to the settlement agreement. Class member claims against Lester were released by the settlement, however.

Lester brought an action against Building Materials in New Mexico state court. Lester sought damages for breach of contract, breach of express and implied warranties, fraud and loss of business reputation as a consequence of having used defective Inner-Seal Siding in its buildings. Lester alleged that it had sold approximately 2,600 buildings with Inner-Seal Siding. Lester further alleged that it "has received and will continue to receive hundreds of claims and complaints ... which must be administered and resolved in order to avoid further losses."

Lester recognized that new claims by class members were foreclosed by the settlement agreement but observed that the settlement "provide[d] no relief or monetary compensation to [Lester], [its] dealers, or others similarly situated." Because its injuries were not redressed by the settlement agreement, Lester asserted that Building Materials was obligated to indemnify Lester for any damages arising from claims by Lester's customers arising from defects in and failure of Building Materials' Inner-Seal.

Building Materials disagreed with Lester's interpretation of the effect of the settlement agreement and moved, in the state court action, for partial summary judgment on all present and future claims against Building Materials related to the failure of Inner-Seal Siding.

The trial court denied the motion and the case was tried. A significant portion of the trial centered on the issue of damages. Lester argued that moral and business compulsions required it to remove and replace the Inner-Seal Siding on every building that it sold, even if the owner of the building had received at least some compensation in the prior settlement with Building Materials.

The defense portion of the case focused on the effect of the class action settlement. Building Materials called an expert witness who testified that, based on a comparison of the list of opt-outs and a list of purchasers of Lester's buildings, none of Lester's customers had opted out of the class action settlement. The expert further asserted that some $640,000 had been paid to Lester's customers from the settlement fund.

Following deliberations, the jury returned a verdict of $29.6 million in favor of Lester.

At this point, Building Materials filed a motion in the federal district court in Oregon claiming that the court had continuing jurisdiction over the settlement. Building Materials asked the district court to enjoin the state court from entering judgment on the portion of the verdict that was inconsistent with the class action settlement.

Question

Which of the exception to the Anti-Injunction Act, if any, will allow the judge to enjoin enforcement of the New Mexico judgment? Why?

Anti-Injunction Act and *Younger* Abstention

Stewart v. Legal Advertising Committee, et als.

Edwin F. Stewart is a New Mexico attorney specializing in estate planning. He regularly presents seminars on creating living trusts and also advises clients on how to structure their assets in order to qualify for Medicaid. He solicits potential clients through print advertising. Until recently, New Mexico attorneys wishing to advertise had to submit potential advertisements to the Legal Advertising Committee ("LAC") for approval prior to public dissemination. If the LAC found that a proposed advertisement violated New Mexico legal advertising regulations it would issue a report to the Disciplinary Board of the Supreme Court of the State of New Mexico if the attorney went ahead and disseminated the advertisement without correction. After receiving a report from the LAC, the Disciplinary Board would have the option to file formal charges against the attorney. If the Disciplinary Board filed formal charges, the Disciplinary Board would also appoint a hearing officer to preside over the proceedings. Following an adverse decision by the hearing officer an attorney could appeal to the full Disciplinary Board and, if unsuccessful, to the New Mexico Supreme Court.

A year ago, the Deputy Chief Disciplinary Counsel of the Disciplinary Board, sent a letter to Mr. Stewart notifying him that the LAC forwarded complaints to her regarding legal advertisements

Stewart had submitted. The letter suggested changes and deletions to the advertisements. The letter also informed Mr. Stewart that if he made the changes he would receive an informal admonition, and if he did not he would face formal disciplinary charges. Instead of responding to the letter, Mr. Stewart filed a federal lawsuit against the LAC, the Disciplinary Board, and the New Mexico Supreme Court. He sought a preliminary injunction forbidding enforcement of the New Mexico advertising rules. He alleged violations of the First Amendment, the Due Process Clause, and the Equal Protection Clause, pursuant to 42 U.S.C. § 1983.

Questions

1. Is there subject matter jurisdiction over Mr. Stewart's federal lawsuit against the LAC, the Disciplinary Board, and the New Mexico Supreme Court? If so, on what basis?

2. At the time Stewart filed the federal complaint, did the Anti-Injunction Act prevent the federal court from issuing an injunction against enforcement of the advertising rules under §1983?

3. At the time Stewart filed the federal complaint, did *Younger* abstention require the federal court to abstain? Why or why not?

4. Assume that shortly after Stewart filed the federal complaint, the Disciplinary Board filed formal charges against Mr. Stewart.

   A. Is there subject matter jurisdiction over Mr. Stewart's federal lawsuit against the LAC, the Disciplinary Board, and the New Mexico Supreme Court?

   B. Does the Anti-Injunction Act now apply to prevent the federal court from issuing an injunction against enforcement of the advertising rules under §1983? Why or why not?

   C. Does *Younger* abstention require the federal court to abstain? Do you need additional facts? What facts do you need? Why?

5. Assume that while the federal court was considering the abstention issue, Mr. Stewart forwarded two new advertisements to the LAC and that the LAC denied Mr. Stewart the right to use these advertisements. The LAC also advised Mr. Stewart that if he did not terminate use of these advertisements he might again face professional discipline. In response, Mr. Stewart filed a petition before the Disciplinary Board seeking declaratory relief and appealing the LAC's denial of these new advertisements. In response, the Disciplinary Board issued an order staying the pending disciplinary proceeding. Do these additional developments change any of your answers to Questions 4A–4C.

Younger Abstention

Triple X Entertainment, Inc. v. City of Columbia

As a result of repeated complaints, local residents in Columbia, South Carolina sought to close down the "Triple X," a local adult bookstore and movie house, on charges that the constant flow of traffic of persons seeking adult-related sexual material created a public nuisance in the surrounding neighborhood. To accomplish this purpose, the city attorney filed a civil complaint in the state trial court seeking a declaration that the building was a "public nuisance" and an order compelling the shutdown of the business. In response, owners of the "Triple X" went to federal court and filed a separate action under the federal Civil Rights act against the city alleging actions by the city violated the First Amendment Constitutional rights of the owners. The owners sought to enjoin the City's presentation of the nuisance claim. For purposes of this question, you must assume that the City has a valid civil nuisance claim and that the owners have a valid claim for breach of their First Amendment rights. The City has moved to stay or dismiss the federal action claiming that the federal court should abstain from exercising subject matter jurisdiction.

Questions

Which of the following accurately describes the position the trial court should take when asked to abstain in the matter? Why?

1. The Federal Court should not hear the claim either because a decision on whether the business is a nuisance is a uniquely state decision thereby implicating *Pullman* abstention or because the City's filing of a nuisance claim suggests a complex state scheme and implicates abstention under the *Burford* abstention doctrine;

2. The Federal Court should not hear the claim because the remedy sought by the Owners of the "Triple X" would violate the Anti-Injunction Act;

3. The Federal Court should not hear the claim because even if permissible under the Anti-Injunction Act, the Court should abstain under the *Younger* doctrine.

Rolfing v. State Board of Surveying Examiners

Samantha Rolfing was a licensed land surveyor in Kent County, Michigan. She was an outspoken critic of the State Board of Surveying Examiners, which, according to Samantha, was overly concerned with the welfare of city, rather than country surveyors like her. She regularly campaigned against the incumbent members of the Board whenever those members were appointed by the state's governor. Some time ago, Davis Halper another surveyor, from one of the state's largest cities, complained to the State Board that Samantha was incompetent. The complaint arose out of surveying done at the state university by both Rolfing, on behalf of one contractor, and Halper, on behalf of another. At her hearing before the State Board, the Chair of the Board told Samantha that because Samantha had been admitted as a surveyor some 25 years before this event, the Board had no measure of her competency. The Chair "suggested" that Samantha take the written examination for surveyor which, the Chair said, would prove her competence. Even though Samantha received the highest score on the written examination of those taking the test, the State Board still revoked her license as a surveyor. Samantha appealed this decision through state administrative procedures, claiming that the real reason for revocation of her license was Samantha's criticism of the state board. She also filed a federal lawsuit, alleging that the state board violated her civil rights. In that suit, Samantha sought damages only against the board and its individual members.

Questions

1. Assuming the state board moves to dismiss this action based on abstention, how should the court rule?
2. Do the tenets of "Our Federalism," which underlie the *Younger* doctrine, apply equally when the federal lawsuit seeks damages rather than injunctive relief?
3. In *Younger* type cases, the federal court dismisses the federal claim seeking to enjoin the state proceeding so as to not interfere with the ongoing state action. If the doctrine applies to damage actions, is dismissal of the federal proceeding still necessary?

Pullman, Burford, Thibodaux Colorado River Abstention

Free State Railway, Inc. v. Public Service Commission

The Montana Public Service Commission is empowered to license, unlicense, regulate and control tariffs upon and otherwise regulate state railroads within the state of Montana. Appeals from decisions by the Public Service Commission go directly to the State Court of Appeals. Free State Railway, a corporation incorporated in Delaware with a principal place of business in Illinois, operates a railroad within Montana. Free State sought permission from the Public Service Commission to discontinue service on a relatively short local railroad route, because, according to Free State, the route was a financial disaster. Responding to several local citizens who occasionally used the route, the Commission refused to allow discontinuance of the route, instead ordering Free State to continue in operation. Following the Commission's decision, attorneys for Free State have filed a federal complaint against the Commission alleging that the Commission's decision constitutes an impermissible taking of Free State's property, in violation of the 5th Amendment to the Federal Constitution and further that the Commission's decision ordering it to continue to operate constitutes an impermissible use of the Commission's power under state law.

Question

The Commission seeks to dismiss/stay the federal lawsuit arguing that the federal court should abstain. Discuss the applicability of the various abstention doctrines.

Starr v. City of New Haven

Alfred and Gina Starr are co-owners of property located on the outskirts of New Haven, Connecticut. Over the past several years, the city of New Haven has cited the Starrs on several occasions for having excessive personal property in their yard and around the house; enough such property to create a nuisance. In fact, the City had given notice that if the violations of the City's housing code were not abated, the City would clean the property itself.

About a month ago, city workers came onto the Starr's property without their permission and without a warrant and began removing personal property from the yard and from within the house.

Gina Starr arrived at the home while the City was removing her property and demanded that the City cease and desist. When the City refused, Gina went to an attorney who obtained a temporary restraining order in state court. That TRO has now been turned into a preliminary injunction. The action underlying the request for injunction remains pending in state court. In that action, the Starrs seek to permanently enjoin the City from entering upon their property. This claim is predicated on the allegation that state law does not authorize the type of nuisance the City has claimed applies to the Starr's property.

The Starr's also filed an action in the appropriate federal district court under 42 U.S.C. § 1983, claiming that the City's warrantless entry into their home and its removal of the plaintiffs' personal property was a violation of the Fourth Amendment of the Constitution.

Questions

1. Is there federal subject matter jurisdiction over the Starr's federal court action? Why or why not?

2 Is *Younger* abstention applicable to prohibit the federal court

from hearing the federal action?

3. Are there unsettled questions of state law applicable to the state proceeding?

4. Assuming there are unsettled questions of state law, should they require the federal court to abstain under *Pullman*? Why or why not?

5. Does the federal claim involve an inquiry into a state regulatory scheme?

6. Assuming there will be an inquiry into the state regulatory scheme, should the federal court abstain under *Burford*? Why or why not?

7. Are there any other basis for federal court abstention?

8. If there are not, how can the federal case proceed while the state case is also proceeding?

CHAPTER 4

THE ERIE DOCTRINE

The General Rule

VanDam v. Speedie Mart, Inc.

Alice VanDam is a citizen of the State of Maine. While visiting her Mother in New Jersey, Alice fell on ice at the Speedie Mart near her Mother's home. The Speedie Mart knew about the ice, but refused to do anything about it. It even refused to warn incoming patrons about the problem. Speedie Mart is a national corporation, incorporated in Delaware, with its principal place of business in New York. It has a chain of stores in most states, including Maine. Speedie Mart does a systematic and continuous business in each of these states. A good estimate of Alice's damages is that she has about $100,000 worth of provable medical, wage and pain and suffering claims. Assume Alice files a federal diversity action in the federal district court in Maine.

Questions

1. What rules of procedure will be used in this case? Why?
2. What substantive law will be used in this case? Why?
3. How will the court determine what substantive law will be used in this case?
4. Suppose the case were originally filed in state court in Maine and removed by Speedie Mart based on diversity of citizenship. Would any of your answers change?

Sharon J. Corporation v. Langworthy

The Sharon J Corporation sued Daniel Langworthy in the United States District court for Alabama. The claim alleged that Langworthy improperly used a song written by country legend Hank Williams in advertising for Langworthy's used car business. Sharon J. Corporation owns the copyright to this song and the suit is brought pursuant to 28 U.S.C. §1338.

Question

Is this an *Erie* question? Why or why not?

State Statute/Rule v. Federal Rule

Shannon Health Corp. v. Salem Carpet Corp.

Salem Carpet Corporation, a corporate citizen of Idaho entered into a $1 million agreement with Shannon Health Corporation whereby Salem would provide and install new carpeting to the Shannon Health hospital facility, located in Shannon's corporate home of Utah. After the contract was entered into, Salem contracted with Centrex Installers, Inc., another corporate citizen of Idaho to perform the actual installation of the Shannon Health carpet under Salem's direction.

After installation of the carpet went very badly, Shannon Health Corporation sued Salem Carpet Corporation in federal court in Idaho, alleging in negligence both that the carpeting was defective and that it was defectively installed. Salem Carpet Corporation denied that the carpeting was defective. It also denied that the carpeting was defectively installed and alleged that any defect in installation was entirely the fault of Centrex Installers. Salem Carpet then filed a third party claim against Centrex as a third party defendant under Federal Rule of Civil Procedure 14. Salem sought an apportionment of Centrex's fault under applicable state law and a finding that Centrex alone was the cause of any damage suffered by Shannon Health. Idaho state law provided that an entity may be joined as a third party if it "caused or contributed to the damages for which recovery is sought." Centrex moved to dismiss the third party claim. It alleged that under Fed. R. Civ. P. 14, it can only be joined if Centrex is or may be liable to Salem Carpet, not if Centrex is liable to Shannon Medical for its damages, as would be the case under the statute. You must assume for this question that both of these interpretations are correct under Rule 14 and the Idaho statute

Questions

1. If this case is decided using only *Erie* as precedent, what result? Why?

2. If this case is decided using only *Guaranty Trust* as precedent, what result? Why?

3. If this case is decided using only *Hanna v. Plumer* as precedent, what result? Why?

Allen v. The Condominiums at Argyle, Inc.

Michelle Allen is a citizen of Wyoming. The Condominiums at Argyle, Inc. is a Utah corporation which built and sells condominium units at a popular Utah vacation spa, Argyle Falls. Michelle Allen purchased a vacation condominium in a development built by Condominiums. The public and common areas of the condominium were to be maintained by the Argyle Condominium Association, another Utah corporation. Shortly after taking possession of her unit, Michelle Allen detected a persistent, unpleasant odor in her unit. The Association deemed Allen's complaints to be unfounded and refused to participate in investigation or repair of the situation. Eventually, Allen vacated her unit. Following further discussions with Condominium's insurer, an investigation was conducted, revealing construction defects in the common areas of the unit that were resulting in the release of sewer gas inside the unit. Allen maintains that neither Condominiums or the Association remedied the defect, and that her demands upon the insurance company to do so were neither reasonably investigated or paid.

Allen filed suit in an appropriate federal district court against both Condominiums and the Association. She alleged breach of contract, both assault and a separate battery (because of her exposure to sewer gas), breach of fiduciary duty against the Association, and several other claims. She sought damages to compensate her for personal injuries, for loss of the use of her condominium unit and exemplary or punitive damages to punish Condominiums and the Association. The Association has moved to dismiss Allen's demand for exemplary damages. Under applicable state law, which is included in the state rules of civil procedure and which you may assume is true, a claim for exemplary damages may not be included in an initial pleading, but rather, may only be asserted following discovery and amendment of the pleading to assert the basis for the demand. Michelle Allen argues that because the matter is in federal court, Rule 9(g) requires only that she plead punitive damages specifically, which you may assume she did.

Questions

1. If this case is decided using only *Erie* as precedent, what

result? Why?

    2. If this case is decided using only *Guaranty Trust* as precedent, what result? Why?

    3. If this case is decided using only *Hanna v. Plumer* as precedent, what result? Why?

State Judicial Ruling v. Federal Rule

Columbia Mutual Ins. Co. v. New Line Technologies, Inc.

    New Line Technologies Inc. is a Florida corporation which manufactured and sold asbestos-containing side boards and rings which were used to maximize temperature during the steel manufacturing process. Columbia Mutual Insurance Company is a Missouri insurance corporation that writes all of the liability insurance for New Line. New Line Technologies has been named as a defendant in numerous lawsuits initiated by steel workers who allege that they have suffered bodily injury as a result of exposure to New Line's asbestos-containing products. Columbia Mutual paid judgments and/or settlements on behalf of New Line Technologies in excess of $5,000,000, the total coverage available under its Columbia Mutual primary liability policies. Columbia Mutual then advised New Line that claims had reached the policy limits and refused to defend or pay any additional claims. New Line disagreed claiming that there was additional coverage and demanded that Columbia Mutual continue to defend and pay claims. Columbia then filed suit in an appropriate Florida federal district court against New Line seeking a declaration that Columbia was no longer obligated to defend or pay on these lawsuits. That lawsuit is pending. Carl Johnson is a citizen of Alabama and was employed as a steel worker at the Birmingham Steel Company. Johnson filed suit against New Line for the injuries he suffered as a result of exposure to New Line produced asbestos. Johnson's lawsuit was filed after Columbia Mutual alleged that the New Line policy limits had been exhausted. Johnson moves, pursuant to Federal civil procedure rule 24 to be allowed to join the *Columbia Mutual v. New Line* federal lawsuit, in Florida, so as to protect his ability to potentially collect damages from the insurance company. For the sake of this problem, you may assume that prior federal decisions have uniformly ruled that a mere financial interest, such as Johnson has, is not the kind of legally protected interest necessary to join a federal lawsuit. Additionally, because Johnson has no direct interest in the *Columbia Mutual v. New Line* lawsuit in that he is not a beneficiary or an owner of the policy, his chances of joining the lawsuit under Rule 24 are, at best, remote. Johnson, however, argues that a Florida state court decision requires that, in a declaratory judgment action by an insurer against an insured, all those having claims against the insured are indispensable parties and must be joined in the lawsuit. Johnson claims that this interpretation of state law requires that he be joined.

Questions

1. If this case is decided using only *Erie* as precedent, what result? Why?

2. If this case is decided using only *Guaranty Trust* as precedent, what result? Why?

3. If this case is decided using only *Hanna v. Plumer* as precedent, what result? Why?

State Statute v. Federal Case Law

Arneze v. Directory National Bank

Amanda Arneze, a citizen of New Mexico, was employed with the Directory National Bank, a corporate citizen of Illinois, in Directory National's Gallup, NM branch office. Alleging that the bank systematically discriminated against her on several grounds, Arneze filed suit in New Mexico state court alleging violations of both Title VII of the Federal Civil Rights Act, and substantially similar provisions of the New Mexico Civil Rights Act. After the action was filed, Directory National removed the action to federal court. Well into this action, Directory National Bank served Arneze with a settlement proposal according to New Mexico statute. For the purpose of this problem only, you should assume there is such a statute and that it provides:

> In any civil action for damages filed in the courts of this state, if a defendant files an offer of judgment which is not accepted by the plaintiff within 30 days, the defendant shall be entitled to recover reasonable costs and attorney's fees incurred by her or him ... from the date of filing of the offer if the judgment is one of no liability ...

Arneze did not accept Directory National Bank's settlement proposal, and about six weeks after Directory National Bank served its proposal, the Court granted Summary Judgment in Directory National Bank's favor. Directory National Bank now seeks an order requiring Arneze to pay $38,277.65 in attorney's fees Directory National Bank purportedly accrued since service of its proposal. Arneze contends that she should not be held liable for Directory National Bank's attorney's fees, in relevant part, because the action is largely one sounding in federal law and, under *Christiansburg Garment Co. v. EEOC,* 434 U.S. 412, 98 S.Ct. 694, 54 L.Ed.2d 648 (1978), the Supreme Court determined the standard by which a prevailing defendant in a Title VII case can recover attorney's fees from a plaintiff. In the case, the Court reaffirmed The American Rule whereby litigants must pay their own fees, unless a litigant has proceeded in bad faith or a relevant statute provides for fee shifting. The Court held that Title VII permitted a prevailing defendant to recover fees only if a plaintiff's claim proves frivolous, unreasonable, or groundless, or the plaintiff continued to litigate after the claim clearly became so. Arneze argued that there is no such showing in this case and, indeed, both sides agree that there is no allegation that Arneze's claim was frivolous, unreasonable, or groundless.

Questions

1. If this case is decided using only *Erie* as precedent, what result? Why?

2. If this case is decided using only *Guaranty Trust* as precedent, what result? Why?

3. If this case is decided using only *Hanna v. Plumer* as precedent, what result? Why?

4. How important to your answers is it that the case is being decided under the Federal Civil Rights Law, rather than the identical state Civil Rights provision?

Camacho v. Texas Workforce Comm.

Sonja Camacho, Arnold Sequoia, and Ellen Banter, among others were, at one time, recipients of Medicaid health care coverage. The Medicaid program is a federal program operated at the state level by a state commission. When the Texas Workforce Commission, the state agency empowered to administer the statewide Medicaid program, changed eligibility standards, thereby excluding Comacho, Sequoia and Banter, as well as the others, they sued the Workforce Commission in state court, seeking a declaratory judgement of eligibility. The Texas Workforce Commission properly removed the matter to federal court, asserting federal question jurisdiction. After the district court invalidated the rules at issue, holding them contrary to federal law, Camacho, Sequoia, and Banter filed an application for attorney's fees in the district court. The Texas Declaratory Judgment Act, under which the suit was filed provides: "In any proceeding under this chapter, the court may award costs and reasonable and necessary attorney's fees as are equitable and just." The Texas Workforce Commission argues that the Declaratory Judgment Act is a procedural statute that does not apply in federal court. Rather, they argue, the federal court must follow the traditional federal court mandate known as The American Rule requiring all parties in federal court to pay their own attorney fees.

Questions

1. If this case is decided using only *Erie* as precedent, what result? Why?

2. How should a federal court decide if an issue is substantive or procedural?

3. If this case is decided using only *Guaranty Trust* as precedent, what result? Why?

4. If this case is decided using only *Hanna v. Plumer* as precedent, what result? Why?

What State Law is Used–Klaxon and *Erie*

Kaiser v. Tiger Properties, Inc.

Montgomery and Francis Kaiser were married in Belgium where they were both citizens. They then moved to Freeport, Grand Bahamas. Thereafter, Francis Kaiser flew to Mississippi. Two days later, she filed for divorce from Montgomery in Mississippi state court. The state court held that Mr. and Ms. Kaiser were domiciled in Mississippi for purposes of divorce proceedings in that state. It entered a divorce decree and later appointed Margaret Deland as a receiver "to manage, control, and preserve the property" of the marital estate. Determining what assets belonged to the marital estate became a hotly contested matter involving extensive litigation in many jurisdictions. Tiger Properties, Inc., is a Liberian corporation that owns real estate in a number of countries, including the United States. Francis Kaiser reasonably believed that real property ostensibly owned by Tiger Properties in Idaho, valued at over $1 million, should be included in the marital estate and, with the help of Margaret Deland, filed suit in state court in Idaho asserting this claim. Tiger removed the case to an appropriate Idaho federal court based on diversity. In the federal court, Tiger Properties filed a third party claim against Deland. Tiger's central contention against Deland was that she engaged in tortious abuse of process in assisting Ms. Kaiser in bringing the Idaho suit against Tiger and was, as a result, liable to Tiger Properties for any damages owed to Ms. Kaiser. Deland did not address the validity of this third party claim under Rule 14, but instead moved for summary judgment in the federal district court based on a defense of official immunity as a court-appointed receiver.

For purposes of this problem, you should assume that Federal law, Idaho state law, and Mississippi each have separate doctrines of immunity for court officers, although each applies their own standards for judging these claims.

Questions

1. What standard should the court use in determining whether state or federal law governs Deland's claim of immunity?

2. Assuming for the purpose of this question only that the court determines that state law applies, which state's law should the court apply to Deland's claim of immunity?

CHAPTER 5

PLEADINGS AND MOTIONS

Accrual of a Cause of Action

Knight v. deVries, Jones & Associates

Knight Advertising, owned by Darnell Knight, employed the law firm of deVries, Jones and Associates to represent them in litigation against a former employee, Eric Johnson. Knight Advertising sought to enforce a covenant not to compete against Johnson and to sue to recover the amounts due in connection with Johnson's alleged default on a loan from Knight.

On behalf of Knight, Lawyer Amanda Jones filed an action in South Carolina state court in connection with the alleged loan. Although Knight was unable to produce the original promissory note, he produced a "copy" which Jones attached to the petition and which Jones used to obtain an order authorizing the seizing of Johnson's automobile to satisfy the outstanding amount left on the loan. Soon thereafter, however, Lawyer Jones learned that the note submitted to the court was not a copy but was a new document that Knight had created shortly before the action was filed.

deVries and Jones summoned Knight to their office in Georgia, confronted him with the information, asked Knight to sign a statement telling the truth and indicated that deVries and Jones would no longer represent Knight, although they would .attempt to negotiate a settlement with Johnson and Johnson's attorney.

The next day, Amanda Jones called Knight to notify him of proposed terms of a settlement between Knight and Johnson.   There followed several telephone conversations related to the proposed settlement. During their second or third of these phone conversations, Knight tentatively agreed to accept the settlement terms.   In the meantime, Knight consulted with another attorney because he was concerned that Amanda Jones and her firm were no longer acting in Knight's best interest. Knight felt that he was being asked to capitulate to Johnson as a result of what he perceived to be deVries and Jones' mishandling of the case. Proof of his capitulation came when Knight saw in writing the proposed settlement which called upon Knight to dismiss all litigation against Johnson with prejudice.   It also provided that Knight would forfeit the $10,000 bond Knight posted to attach Johnson's car to Johnson, return the automobile to Johnson and assume all costs associated with its seizure. Additionally, Knight was to pay Johnson his final wages, withdraw any opposition to Johnson's claims for unemployment compensation, and cancel Johnson's employment contract, including the covenant not to compete.

Through new counsel, Knight filed a legal malpractice action against deVries, Jones, and their firm in South Carolina state court. After Knight's attorney in the malpractice action withdrew, Knight did not obtain replacement counsel or appear at a scheduled hearing, and the court dismissed the case without prejudice.

Because the matter was dismissed without prejudice thereby allowing another action to be filed, Knight filed the same malpractice action, this time in Georgia state court.

Questions

In his book *Civil Procedure* 335 (Aspen 6th ed. 2004), author Stephen Yeazell indicates that a legal claim requires two elements: a body of law, such as tort or contract that allows the claim and a set of facts that fits within that law.

1. At what point in these facts were both of those requirements met?

2. When is the answer to when these requirements are met most likely to be important? Why?

RULE 11

Nichols v. Deacon

Albert Nichols sues Elisa Deacon in federal court alleging diversity of citizenship. Albert claims that Deacon negligently ran into Albert with a motor vehicle. At the time of the filing of the complaint, Albert's investigation had produced no actual evidence of Deacon's negligence, however, Albert, and Albert's lawyer, were confident their interview of Calahan, a witness to the accident, would produce such evidence. Calahan had been unavailable for interview prior to the filing of the complaint. In the complaint, Albert pleaded that "Deacon negligently collided with Albert."

Questions

1. After the case was settled with Deacon paying Albert $60,000, Deacon filed a motion claiming Albert's complaint violated Rule 11. Discuss.

2. Assume that Deacon did not file a motion claiming Albert's complaint violated Rule 11. After hearing testimony in the case, however, the judge believed that Albert's complaint was in violation of the rule. Can the judge file a Rule 11 complaint? What is it about Rule 11 that allows the judge to become a "participant" in the litigation in this way?

3. Who decides if there has been a Rule 11 violation? Is that true even if the judge initiates the proceeding?

3. Assuming there is a violation of Rule 11, what are the available sanctions? What should be the sanction for this violation? Why?

Hartwig v. Estes & Estate of Farren

Lisa Hartwig, a citizen of Tennessee, sued Marvin Estes and the Estate of Harold Farren, both citizens of Illinois, claiming that either Estes or Farren was driving a motor vehicle that struck Hartwig's vehicle. The case was based on diversity of citizenship. Hartwig's complaint alleged damages in the amount of $100,000. Estes' attorney was aware that Estes was driving the motor vehicle that struck Hartwig, but knows that Hartwig cannot prove this because Farren is already dead and there are no other witnesses to this accident. In an answer filed in the matter, Estes' lawyer therefore denied that Estes was driving the motor vehicle. After the foregoing facts are shown at trial, the court, on its own motion, under Rule 11, directs Estes' attorney to show cause why the attorney should not be sanctioned under that Rule.

Question

Argue either side of the case—either in favor of sanction or on behalf of Estes' lawyer.

Debard v. SaveALot Corporation

Lawyer James Johnson is a lawyer admitted in Arizona. Johnson obtained a federal court judgment in favor of his client Carolyn Debard who was assaulted outside a Prescott, Arizona SaveALot store. The judgment was against SavALot Corporation for $1.5 million dollars for failing to provide security at the store. After receiving the judgment, Lawyer Johnson presented to the trial judge a paper entitled "Writ of Execution" designed to compel SavALot, as a party, to deliver money or property to the sheriff. The judge signed the writ against SavALot and, although this writ is usually served by the local sheriff, and would normally be served on SavALot's registered agent in Phoenix, Johnson elected to serve the warrant himself on the local SavALot store where the assault took place. Johnson called all the local television media and had them accompany him to the SavALot store, taping and then playing on the evening news the fact that Johnson thought it necessary to serve the warrant on SavALot personally, because of fear that the defendant would not have money to pay the judgment.

Questions

1. SavALot has filed an application for Rule 11 sanctions against Lawyer Johnson. Be prepared to argue either that sanctions should or should not be awarded in favor of SavALot and the reasons for your answer.

2. Can you make an argument that sanctions should be mandatory in certain cases? When? What role does the "safe harbor" provision play in your answer?

Merced v. State

Dennis Spitzer has been licensed to practice law in South Carolina for 20 years. In the spring, four years ago, Spitzer represented Alton Merced, an inmate at the state's McCormick Correctional Institution. On behalf of Merced, Spitzer filed suit against the state claiming that Merced had been assaulted on numerous occasions by both guards and other inmates at McCormick. The gravamen of the complaint was that the alleged beatings and stabbing had left Mr. Merced paralyzed, and confined to a wheelchair. The office of the attorney general of South Carolina defended the case. In a motion for summary judgment in the case of Merced v. State, deputy attorney general Joanne McCabe, who was the primary attorney general in the case, presented the affidavit of Dr. Harry Coyle, the medical director of the McCormick Correctional Institution. In that affidavit, which was attached to the motion, Dr. Coyle stated:

   1. She had discussed the Merced v. State case extensively with Dennis Spitzer, attorney for Mr. Merced;

   2. Dennis Spitzer asked Coyle to be prepared to testify to Mr. Merced's medical injuries;

   3. Spitzer told Coyle not to worry about giving an opinion–that Spitzer anticipated getting a big settlement from the State, and that if Coyle played his cards right, Coyle could have a "big chunk" of the fee, and could probably retire;

   4. Despite the claim that Merced was paralyzed, Dr. Coyle had seen Merced, on several occasions, move his legs and stand.

   The trial judge dismissed the case, based, in part, on the Coyle affidavit. Thereafter, Dennis Spitzer filed a federal suit for violation of the constitutional rights of Merced against attorney general Joanne McCabe, and the State. The gist of that suit was that the affidavit was untruthful and consisted of defamatory material. That suit was summarily dismissed after the state showed that the affidavits upon which the defamation case was based were filed in a judicial proceeding and were, therefore, privileged. Upon dismissal of the defamation case, the state then sought Rule 11 sanctions against Dennis Spitzer.

Questions

   1. Assume that the federal court believes that it must follow state law on whether documents are privileged. The state's highest court has held, in numerous published opinions, that the filing of a document in a legal proceeding is absolutely privileged.

   a. Are sanctions under Rule 11 appropriate against Spitzer?

   b. Does the immunity of papers filed in judicial proceedings tell you anything about the need for procedural remedies such as Rule 11?

   2. Assume that the state's highest court had not ruled on the privilege extended to documents filed in judicial proceedings, but that the highest courts of a number of other influential states had held such documents absolutely privileged. Are Rule 11 sanctions appropriate against Spitzer?

   3. Assume that the state's highest court had not ruled on the privilege extended to documents filed in judicial proceedings, but that

one of the intermediate appellate courts of the state had ruled such documents absolutely privileged, while another intermediate appellate court of the state had ruled that such documents are not privileged. Are Rule 11 sanctions appropriate against Spitzer?

Pleading Jurisdiction of the Court

Thiel v. Central State University

Greta Thiel, is a citizen of the nation of Uruguay. She married Rudolf Thiel, another citizen of Uruguay in the state of Massachusetts while Rudolf Thiel was a resident of the United States on permanent resident status. When Rudolf Thiel's job transferred him to the State of Georgia, Greta also moved to Georgia. There, she enrolled in and subsequently completed the Center for English as a Second Language program at Georgia's Central State University, a public university. She then applied for student enrollment at CSU as an international student and was accepted. After residing in Georgia for six months, Greta sought status as an in-state resident for tuition purposes in the nursing program at Central State University. University officials denied her application. The University's denial of in-state tuition status was based on its construction of the state's Department of Higher Education's "Residency Classification for Tuition Purposes by Public Colleges and Universities." Pursuant to these regulations, "[a] student should be classified as an instate student for tuition purposes only if his or her legal residence is located in Georgia." According to the University, Ms. Thiel could not meet these qualifications because she was present in the United States on an international student visa.

Greta Thiel filed suit against Central State University in federal district court. Her complaint does not contain a paragraph substantially similar to Form 2 of the Forms contained in the Federal Rules of Civil Procedure. Her complaint does contain the following language:

1. That by adopting the rules and regulations whereby a legal resident and domiciliary of the State of Georgia can be denied recognition as a resident of the State of Georgia for tuition and registration purposes, the defendant has attempted to assume or usurp powers vested only in the legislature of the State of Georgia under its constitutional authority. Said rules and regulations are without any legal effect since they were enacted without any power or authority;

2. That the rules and regulations constitute an infringement on the freedom of movement protected by the Privileges and Immunities clause of the 14th

Amendment of the United States Constitution;

3.   That the rules and regulations constitute an unreasonable and invidiously discriminatory classification and, therefore, are a denial of the equal protection of laws under the 14th Amendment of the United States Constitution;

4. That the rules and regulations place a discriminatory burden on an alien resident lawfully within the United States and conflict with the constitutionally derived federal power to regulate immigration in violation of the Supremacy Clause of the U.S. Constitution;

5. That the rules and regulations constitute a violation of the due process, equal protection and immunity clauses of the Constitution of the State of Georgia; and

6. That defendants exceeded and abused their discretion by denying the plaintiff's claim for registration as a resident of the State of Georgia; that the decision was erroneous and contrary to law, and the entire process was arbitrary and unjust.

Question

Central State University moves to dismiss the complaint for failure to plead a simple and concise statement of jurisdiction under Rule 8(a)(1). What result? Why?

Pleading a Claim

Abrams v. City of Bethany Springs Police Department, et als.

Alden Abrams is a former police officer in the City of Bethany Springs, New Jersey. The city is one of the outer suburbs of New York City. Abrams was dismissed from the police force, subsequently obtained employment with the city Board of Education, but was fired from that employment as well. He has filed a federal court complaint against the City, the City's Police Department and Board of Education, and the appointed heads of each. Abrams' demands for relief are based on the following accusations, among others: religious discrimination; harassment; termination without due process of law; retaliation infringing on free speech rights; failure to issue a gun permit; false arrest; surveillance of plaintiff in the United States and Israel by the City Police Department's Intelligence Division; malicious prosecution and abuse of process; defamation; personal injury as a result of gang warfare that occurred on a "pre-arranged" assignment by the police department; insider trading, prostitution, sexual exploitation and narcotics between Delaney Brothers Investments, Inc., a prominent investment brokerage firm in downtown Bethany Springs and the police department, which, according to plaintiff, is "an effective subsidiary" of Delaney Brothers; and violation of freedom of information rights. Abrams bases federal jurisdiction on violations of the federal civil rights laws, Constitutional violations under the First, Second, Fourth and Fourteenth Amendments; and violation of rights under the Freedom of Information Act. He seeks, in addition to monetary relief, reinstatement and back pay, a declaratory judgment as to his rights, a permanent injunction restraining defendants from maintaining a discriminatory policy against Orthodox Jewish persons and class certification. The class which plaintiff asserts he represents is composed of all Orthodox Jewish persons who are or might be employed by any of the defendants. The complaint is 154 pages long, one paragraph of which reads as follows:

> This complaint also seeks the restitution of the Plaintiff to his employment as Police Officer with full and continuous back pay, pension and restitution for his loss of wages, punitive damages to the Plaintiff by the defendants for the continuous unconstitutional deprivation of rights intentionally instituted by the Defendants, to provide restitution for the entire class of persons which is unduly damaged and perpetuated by the lack of Orthodox Jewish Appearance within the employment of the Police Department and effective discrimination therewith where there is an undue disproportionate number of orthodox Jewish Police Officers which barely number less than ten as a result of an Antisemitic Policy of the City which permeates each and every aspect of law enforcement to the detriment and damage of Orthodox Jewish Persons living in the City and has a rippling effect in cases of Antisemitic lawlessness which currently cost, have cost, and will cost billions of dollars to the Community at large: to wit the bombing of the World Trade Center and the patent, intentional ignorance of the Murder of a World renown Orthodox Jewish leader.

Questions

1. Assuming the court is going to rule that this paragraph (as well as other parts of the Complaint) do not satisfy Rule 8(a), be prepared to discuss why, specifically, the paragraph violates that rule.

2. How would you rewrite the paragraph so as to make it comply with Rule 8(a).

Rule 12 Questions

Collins v. Harper

Myra Collins sues Benedict Harper in a federal court. Harper files no motions addressed to the complaint. Harper does, however, serve an answer containing denials and affirmative defenses but omitting an objection that the court lacks personal jurisdiction over Harper. Nineteen days after serving the answer, Harper serves an amended answer in which the personal jurisdiction objection is raised along with Harper's other defenses.

Question

Would a court be correct if it hears Harper on the issue of lack of personal jurisdiction? Why or why not?

Failure to State a Claim

Welcome to America, Inc. v. McFarland

Jonetta McFarland is the duly appointed Commissioner of the Immigration and Naturalization Service, an agency of the government of the United States. Welcome to America, Inc. (WAI) is a Pennsylvania corporation with its main office in Pittsburgh. Helena Montero, a citizen of Pennsylvania, is the president and CEO of WAI. WAI provides fingerprinting and photography services for immigrants, in two permanent offices and a mobile recreational vehicle which Montero routinely parks in front of the Immigration and Naturalization Service (INS) district office in Pittsburgh. Applicants for various types of immigration benefits must submit fingerprints with their application. The INS then sends the fingerprints to the Federal Bureau of Investigation which checks to see if the applicant has a criminal history, thereby rendering the applicant ineligible for benefits. In the past, INS district offices were responsible for fingerprinting all applicants. However, because available funding dwindled and the number of applications increased, outside providers have recently assumed the majority of the fingerprinting services. Pursuant to an investigation by the Department of Justice's Office of Inspector General, which uncovered problems regarding fingerprint quality, the INS decided to regulate the fingerprinting process. As a result, the INS proposed a regulation, which it publicized in the Federal Register. Among other requirements, the proposed regulation stated that the fingerprinting service must "[m]aintain clean and suitable facilities that are accessible to the general public." When the public comment period ended, the INS waited almost one full year and then, without further notice or comment adopted the proposed rule as final. The final rule required that regulated facilities "[m]aintain permanent clean and suitable facilities that are accessible to the general public" and defined, for the first time, "permanent clean and suitable facilities" as follows. "The use of the term permanent facility shall not include business or organizational operations in private homes, vans or automobiles, mobile cars, and removable stands or portable storefronts."

The attorney for Welcome to America, Inc. then wrote a letter to the INS inquiring whether a new round of public commentary would occur arguing that adding a definition of "facilities" which excluded the operation of vans was a material changes from the proposed regulation, which, under federal law, required a new period for public comment. The INS did not respond to the letter. Thereafter, when Welcome to America, Inc. applied for certification of two permanent offices and its mobile facility, the INS district office denied the application for certification of the mobile facility.

Welcome to America, Inc. then filed suit seeking injunctive relief and declaratory relief against the United States alleging that the actions of the INS in changing the proposed rule without an opportunity for further public comment was "arbitrary, capricious, an abuse of discretion, and otherwise not in accordance with the law." The complaint also alleged that the INS' action was "contrary to constitutional right, power, privilege, or immunity," and that the INS acted in excess of its statutory authority, and that the INS failed to observe the procedures required by law.

Questions

1. Suppose the United States did not answer, but instead filed a motion to dismiss for failure to state a claim under Rule 12(b)(6). What standard should the court use in ruling on this motion?

2. Assume, instead that the United States did answer and then filed a motion to dismiss for failure to state a claim and for judgment on the pleadings. Are there any problems in filing both motions at the same time? What is the difference between the two.

3. Assume that Welcome to America, Inc. also files a motion for judgment on the pleadings. What should the court do now?

4. When must a motion for judgment on the pleadings be filed?

5. Assume that, at the hearing on these motions, the attorney for the INS indicates that the Service has had complaints about Welcome to American, Inc. mobile service and that there are independent grounds for denying them certification. The attorney agrees that this information is not contained in its responsive pleading. The court is willing to consider such evidence and asks that it be submitted in affidavit form by qualified

representatives of the Service.   Can the court consider these issues? How?

More Definite Statements

Regents Hotel Corp. v. Heritage Hotel Corp. et al.

Regents Hotel, Corporation is a Delaware corporation with its principal place of business in Little Rock, Arkansas. Regents is engaged in the business of operating, managing, and franchising hotels. Heritage Hotel Corporation is a Colorado corporation with its principal place of business located in Seattle, Washington; Heritage and Regents are competitors in the hotel industry. Ingrid Helmut is a German citizen; Helmut is a former employee of Regents and the current Chief Executive Officer of Heritage. Business Products, Inc. is an Arkansas corporation with its principal place of business located in Little Rock, Arkansas. Business Products assisted both Regents and Heritage in administering travel-related marketing programs.

In this action in a proper United States District Court, Regents claims it developed an innovative marketing system known as the "Look to Book" program.   Under this program, travel agents who make travel-related reservations with Regents receive credits which are redeemable for incentive prizes. After the "Look to Book" program was developed, Regents was issued a United States Patent for it.

Ingrid Helmet was a "high-level employee" for Regents during the development of its "Look to Book" incentive program. She allegedly became familiar with the operation of this program, and "gained access to a broad range of Regents proprietary and trade secret information, including marketing and strategy information related to the 'Look to Book' system." Regents now claims that, upon her arrival at Heritage, Helmut wrongfully used the information acquired at Regents's to assist Heritage in developing a competing travel counselor incentive program, referred to as "Heritage Communications."   Heritage is now using this program.

In its suit, Regents alleged that the Heritage incentive program infringed upon the Regents patent for its "Look to Book" program. Other claims were set out in Counts II–IV.

In Count II, trade secret misappropriation, Regents alleged that Heritage violated state statute by wrongfully acquiring and using "Regents trade secret and confidential information relating to the 'Look to Book' incentive program, Regent's valued customers, marketing information concerning the 'Look to Book' program, and other trade secret information related to the hospitality business in which Regents and Heritage compete."   In Count III, unfair competition, Regents set forth no additional facts and alleged only that Heritage and Helmut's conduct "constitutes common law unfair competition." In Count IV, breach of contract, Regents realleged the paragraphs of Count II and stated that "Helmut had a contractual duty not to disclose or use Regents' trade secrets or confidential information in any new employment" Additionally, Count II alleged that "Both Heritage and Helmut knew or had reason to know these contractual obligations and therefore either breached or induced the breach of these contractual obligations and that, as a result, Heritage and Helmut were liable to Regents for breach of contract and/or inducement of such breach."

Both Heritage and Helmut claimed that Counts II, III and IV are impermissibly vague and ambiguous under Rule 12(e)

Questions

1. Are the averments of Counts II, III and IV vague?
2. Assuming they are, how should that vagueness be resolved? Is a requirement for a more definite statement under Rule 12(e) the answer?

Motion to Strike

MCD Media, Inc. v. Tiger Broadcasting, Inc.

MCD Media, Inc. is a British corporation. Tiger Broadcasting, Inc. is a Delaware corporation. Both corporations specialize in the creation and production of entertainment for television, radio and other media. Some time ago, MCD Media developed, for British television a show called "Spouse Swap," a show that centers "on the idea of switching spouses from disparate families and watching the ensuing interactions." More recently, Tiger Broadcasting, Inc. developed a show called "Take My Wife, Please," a show in which wives with contrasting values and lifestyles exchange spouses and families for ten (10) days. MCD entered into an agreement with one of the three major American television networks to produce an American version of "Spouse Swap," based on the British version, for the American television market. After "Take My Wife, Please" began airing in the United States, however, MCD Media, Inc. filed suit in the proper federal court against Tiger Broadcasting, Inc. The suit alleges copyright infringement, a federal question, along with unfair competition and civil conspiracy. To prove copyright infringement requires "willful" infringement. Among a number of other provisions of the Complaint, MCD Media alleged the following:

- Entertainment industry commentators have reported that "Take My Wife, Please" is a "rip-off" of the British hit "Trading Spouses"

Compl. ¶¶ 9, 31, 35-36;

- Tiger's representatives were well aware of MCD's "Trading Spouses" and they intended to create a show similar to it before MCD could get on the U.S. airwaves; *See* Compl. ¶¶ 22, 36, Ex. A.
- Tiger Broadcasting is "behaving like there's an Emmy category for Most Brazen Ripoff," *Id.* ¶ 32;
- "Take My Wife, Please" is a "carbon copy" of "Trading Spouses" *Id.* ¶ 33;
- "Take My Wife, Please" is a "rush-job rip-off of the popular Brit television mainstay." *Id.* ¶ 34.

Tiger Broadcasting moves to strike all of the foregoing paragraphs alleging that they contain "immaterial, impertinent, or scandalous" information, in violation of Rule 12(f).

Question

What result? Why?

Denials/Defenses

Davis v. Elkins

Erin Davis, a citizen of North Carolina, sued Shad Elkins, a citizen of Kansas, in a proper federal district court, for trespass to property Davis owns in North Carolina. Elkins has a building contracting business and, according to Davis, Elkins' heavy equipment operators drove their machinery over Davis' land, ruining the crops that were then growing on the land, as well as damaging some very valuable walnut trees on the land. In her petition, Davis alleges damages to the property from the trespass in excess of $75,000. Elkins denies the trespass, the case goes through discovery and comes to trial. At trial, Davis proves ownership of the property, having acquired it from Smith, and also proves that Elkins entered onto the property with tractors and backhoes. She then provided pictures of the damage and an expert who indicated the damage to the land was at least $90,000 and that the damage to the crops was approximately $125,000. After Davis rested her case, Elkins sought to prove the existence of an assignment from Smith to Elkins authorizing Elkins to enter onto the land to aid the construction business.

Question

　　　　　If Erin Davis' lawyer objects to this proof, what will be the result? Why?

Affirmative Defenses

In re Colonial Bank Receivership

　　　　　After the commissioner of the department of banking for the Commonwealth of Kentucky declared Colonial Bank of Paducah insolvent pursuant to law, the commissioner appointed the Federal Deposit Insurance Corporation as Colonial Bank's receiver. Thereafter, the FDIC, as appointed receiver, filed an action in the appropriate United States District Court alleging that the former officers and directors of Colonial Bank were negligent, grossly negligent, and breached their fiduciary duties with respect to their management and operation of the failed bank.　Lawyers for the defendants have considered asserting multiple defenses against the FDIC in the action. These defenses include:

> (1) That the FDIC, after being appointed receiver, failed to mitigate damages;
> (2) That the FDIC cannot prove that the loans which are the subject of the FDIC claim cannot be collected;
> (3) That Colonial Bank took reasonable steps to collect the loans before being placed into insolvency;
> (4) That the FDIC was negligent in attempting to collect the target loans;
> (5) That the FDIC should be estopped from seeking any damages from the defendants based upon the FDIC's alleged loss or destruction of loan documents;
> (6) That the FDIC is guilty of conflict of interest in that they have applied funds from some of the target loans to loans by the same debtors with other failed banks;
> (7) That a specific federal statute preempts any common law state or federal claims against these defendants;
> (8) That intervening causes prevented collection of these loans;
> (9) That the officers and directors always dealt fairly with respect to the affairs of the bank;
> (10) That the bank's loans were consistent with prevailing banking practice;
> (11) That there was no personal gain to the defendants;
> (12) That the defendants relied upon the advice of others.

Question

As to each of the listed defenses, state whether they must be pleaded as affirmative defenses, why, and why the others are not affirmative defenses.

Amendments

Larchmoor v. Ford Motor Co.

Elliott and Brenda Larchmoor, husband and wife and citizens of North Carolina, were riding in their Ford sedan. Elliott was driving on a major state highway and had the cruise control engaged at approximately 60 mph, the speed limit. When Elliott Larchmoor tried to slow down the vehicle as he approached an intersection, the vehicle instead speeded up, went over an embankment, crashed, and caused substantial injury to both Brenda and Elliott. The Larchmoors filed suit against Ford Motor Co., a Michigan corporation in the proper United States District court based on diversity and asserted multiple causes of action including: strict liability--product defect; strict liability--failure to warn; breach of implied warranty; negligent manufacture, design, or failure to warn; negligence; failure to recall or retrofit defective design and/or manufacture; fraudulent concealment; and loss of consortium. Approximately two weeks prior to trial, Ford moved to amend its answer to include specifically the defense that the Larchmoors failed to mitigate damages by not using their seat belts. In its motion seeking leave to amend, Ford stated that it did not believe that the amendment was necessary, but "[o]ut of an abundance of caution," still sought the amendment.

Questions

1. Is Ford Motor Co. correct that it does not need to amend to assert the defense that the Larchmoors failed to mitigate by not using their seatbelts? Why or why not?

2. What standard should the court use to determine if Ford should be allowed to amend their answer two seeks prior to trial?

CHAPTER 6

JOINDER, INTERVENTION, SUBSTITUTION, INTERPLEADER, CLASS ACTIONS

Joinder of Claims–Generally

N.J. Mall, Inc. v. Wakefield & Associates & Dennis Grodin

Sometime ago, Dennis Grodin, Charlotte Coleman, and others, created Boardwalk, Ltd, a New Jersey limited partnership, for the purpose of purchasing the TAE Mall shopping center located near Atlantic City, New Jersey. After obtaining short-term initial financing, Boardwalk, Ltd. sought to obtain a long term mortgage and solicited several French investors for this purpose.

The interested French investors requested that Wakefield Associates, an independent appraiser, appraise the TAE Mall property. Upon completion of their own due diligence, two interested French investors incorporated N.J. Mall, Inc. for the purpose of providing a loan to Boardwalk, Ltd. To get capital to make this loan, N.J. Mall, Inc. made an initial public offering of its shares. First Financial, Inc., a New York corporation, was the underwriter of the offering. Pierre LaClare and Francois Debovoise (the "French Investors") individually, collectively, and along with First Financial bought approximately 55 percent of N.J. Mall, Inc.'s shares. Private investors purchased 5 percent of the shares. The remaining shares were not sold and were therefore retained by the underwriter First Financial.

As a developer of the project, Dennis Grodin was named to the Board of Directors of N.J. Mall, Inc.'s Board of Directors and was, in fact, ultimately named Chairman of the Board. According to Grodin, N.J. Mall, Inc., through its Board of Directors, agreed to provide officers' and directors' liability insurance coverage for members of the Board, including Grodin.

The law firm of Coleman and Rice, the law firm in which Charlotte Coleman was a partner, were N.J. Mall, Inc.'s United States lawyers. In this connection, Coleman and Rice drafted, purportedly on N.J. Mall, Inc.'s behalf, a Note and a Mortgage for the loan from N.J. Mall, Inc. to Boardwalk, Ltd. Under the Note, which was in the amount of $49 million, Boardwalk, Ltd. was to make interest payments only for several years, and even then only if Boardwalk had the available cash flow to make these payments. There was no requirement that Boardwalk, Ltd. run the business in a way to maximize the likelihood that such a cash flow would be available. The Note also gave N.J. Mall, Inc. certain rights of control with respect to the TAE Mall.

Since the execution of the loan, the TAE Mall's economic performance has not reached the projections provided by Wakefield & Associates. There has been insufficient cash flow for Boardwalk, Ltd. to pay interest to N.J. Mall, Inc. at the agreed-upon interest rates, resulting in the accrual of large amounts of unpaid interest. When the Note matures, all of this interest will be due and it now appears unlikely that

Boardwalk, Ltd. will be able to pay this interest. In addition, the value of the TAE Mall, as collateral for the Note, will be insufficient to satisfy Boardwalk, Ltd.'s obligation.

In response to these problems, the N.J. Mall, Inc's Board of Directors and the French investors implemented a plan to gain control of the TAE Mall by denying Boardwalk, Ltd. the opportunity to further develop the property, thereby depressing its value and forcing Boardwalk, Ltd. to sell the property to N.J. Mall, Inc. or to another buyer. In keeping with its plan, N.J. Mall, Inc. rejected Boardwalk, Ltd.'s proposals to improve and expand the TAE Mall. Both of these actions were ostensibly done under the provisions of the Note giving N.J. Mall, Inc. certain control over the property. In addition, Dennis Grodin also claimed that First Financial, acting on behalf of the French investors, threatened to sue Grodin and Coleman unless Boardwalk, Ltd. sold the TAE Mall immediately with the proceeds to go entirely to N.J. Mall, Inc. When they refused, N.J. Mall, Inc. removed them from N.J. Mall, Inc.'s Board of Directors.

Even further financial downturns for the property caused N.J. Mall, Inc. To file a Complaint in the United States District Court for the District of N.J. That complaint alleged fraud, breach of fiduciary duty and breach of contract against Wakefield & Associates based on what was alleged to be a faulty appraisal of the Mall property and the same claims against Denis Grodin based on his development of the property.

Questions

1. Grodin filed an Answer to N.J. Mall, Inc.'s Complaint. He also filed a Counterclaim against N.J. Mall, Inc. alleging breach of contract for failure to provide him with officers' and directors' insurance. Is this counterclaim appropriate? What is the issue?

2. Grodin also filed a Third-Party Complaint against the French Investors seeking contribution. Wakefield & Associates filed a Third-Party Complaint against Boardwalk, Ltd. What must these Third-Party Complaints say? How can you conceptualize the facts to make valid Third-Party Complaints?

3. After Grodin filed a Third-Party Complaint against the French Investors for contribution, Boardwalk, Ltd. filed a Crossclaim against the French Investors seeking contribution. What problems exist with this Crossclaim?

4. Should any of these claims be severed and tried separately? What standard should a court use to sever?

Joinder of Claims–Federal Issues

Martin v. Able et als.

Sylvio Martin, a citizen of Indiana, owned a building in which he had his office as an architect. The building was in need of repair and Sylvio hired Aaron Able, a citizen of Ohio, to complete the work. Able had done prior work on Sylvio's building and at Sylvio's home. Able subcontracted some of the building repair work to Carlie Simpson, a citizen of Oklahoma. During a period that Simpson's workers were on the Martin building site, one of Simpson's workers negligently started a fire that caused damage to Martin's building well in excess of $75,000. Martin has filed suit in the proper federal court against Abel and Simpson for the damage to his building. Martin also believes there is some damage caused by Abel's workers at Martin's house. Martin adds a second count to his lawsuit against Abel only for this damage. When the suit is received, Abel files a claim against Martin. Abel's claim is for part of the work done on the office building prior to the fire which Martin had not paid. Abel also has a claim against Simpson arising out of work done by Simpson on a different building site being worked on by Abe, and wants to add this claim to the lawsuit.

Question

Are all of these claims proper in the same lawsuit? Which of them can be joined?

Joinder of Claims--Crossclaims

Walton v. Barton

In February, two years ago, Terri Jo Walton was driving her car out of a parking lot owned by Barton Midway Properties, Sam Barton and Kusum Barton. While driving out of this parking lot, Walton's car struck a car being driven by Deborah Johnson. Deborah Johnson was substantially injured and has sued Terri Jo Walton for those injuries, alleging negligent driving by Terri Jo Walton. Following further investigation, Johnson added Barton Midway Properties, Sam Barton and Kusum Barton as defendants, alleging that the Bartons were negligent in placing an outdoor sign on their property that impeded Walton's vision.

Walton and each of the Barton's filed claims against one another as co-defendants for contribution, indemnification, and apportionment of fault relating to Johnson's injuries. Although Walton was injured in the accident, she did not file any cross-claims relating to her injuries. Johnson's lawsuit was settled, and all of Johnson's claims were dismissed with prejudice.

Walton then sued Barton Midway Properties, Sam Barton and Kusum Barton for personal injuries arising from the accident with Johnson. Her husband joined as plaintiff seeking damages for loss of consortium. The Waltons claimed that the Bartons negligently placed the sign in a location where it impaired Walton's ability to safely exit the parking lot. The Bartons filed motions for summary judgment alleging that Walton failed to join her claims in the first suit and that those claims are now barred under the Rules of Civil Procedure.

Questions

1. The claims that Walton and the Bartons filed against each other in the first lawsuit–what kind of claims are those? Why?
2. Based on your answer to Question 1, were those claims "compulsory?" Why or why not?
3. How should the court rule on the Barton's motion for summary judgment?

Permissive Joinder of Parties

Purson and Hayward v. Missouri Valley Insurance Co.

Clare Purson was employed as a litigation supervisor by Blue Ribbon Insurance Company for nine years until the company was taken over by Missouri Valley Insurance Company, approximately three years ago. Shortly after the takeover in June, three years ago, Purson was given a performance evaluation by Kevin Romer, to whom she reported, and received a general rating of "3" (performance meets expectations). Following the review, Romer counseled Purson on some specific areas of her performance that needed improvement. Purson was placed on a 30-day probationary action plan designed to correct those performance problems. By the end of the third week of the 30-day period, Purson was given the option of taking a demotion to litigation adjuster, or to continue the plan and possibly face termination if her performance did not improve by the end of the period.   Purson opted for the demotion, resulting in a $3,000 reduction in salary, and thereafter reported to Mark Romano. Romano evaluated Purson three months later and rated her at a "3" (performance meets expectations).   In light of the favorable recommendation, Romano recommended Purson for a "spot bonus". The bonus was approved by Romer, but before disbursement, Purson notified the company that she had accepted a position with another insurance company. She was replaced by an employee approximately 20 years her junior.

Ernest Hayward was also employed by Blue Ribbon Insurance Company and had occupied the position of litigation adjuster for 18 years prior to the takeover by Missouri Valley Insurance Company. Hayward reported to Purson, who at that time was still serving as a litigation supervisor. The summer following the takeover, Missouri Valley reorganized the claims department to reflect an "aggressive new philosophy of cost-effective management." As a result of the restructuring, Hayward was transferred from the litigation unit to the appeals unit, with no change in title or pay. Hayward was thereafter evaluated by Romano in September 1996 and was given a rating of "4" (performance does not meet the minimum requirements). The basis for the low rating was Hayward' inability to learn defendant's new computer system as well as his "worst case scenario" approach to claims. No disciplinary action was taken. In October 1996, Hayward retired and accepted an offer with another insurance company. Hayward was replaced by another employee 15 years younger than he was.

Both Purson and Hayward claim, in a lawsuit filed in the Federal District Court that Missouri Valley Insurance Company orchestrated a campaign to remove older employees from the claims department, including a campaign of disparaging remarks and harassment. They claimed that their decisions to leave the company were, in fact, because they were to be discharged and that their alleged performance weaknesses were but a pretext for bringing in a younger claims department. The claim is based on the federal Discrimination in Employment Act.

Question

Missouri Valley Insurance Company has moved to severe the two claims alleging that the claims by Purson and Hughes are misjoined because they have neither common questions of law or fact and do not arise from the same transaction or occurrence. What result? Why?

Gallagher v. Leopold, Inc. & Unitruck, Inc.
Gallagher v. Small & Hamilton

The facts for this problem are set out under Removal Problems.

Assume that after the *Gallagher v. Leopold and Garfield* action was removed, Andrea Gallagher moved, under Rule 20, to join Johnson Small and Royson Hamilton to the *Gallagher v. Leopold and Garfield* action.

Questions

1. Are the claims of negligently running the stop sign against Small, the claim of negligently failing to keep his truck under control, and the product liability claims of defective design against Leopold and Garfield the same claims at law?

2. If they are not, will Rule 20(a) allow their joinder? Why or why not?

3. Can the claim against Small and Johnson be joined in this federal court proceeding? Why or why not?

4. Under 28 U.S.C. §1447(e), what should the federal court do?

Permissive Joinder of Parties– Third Party Claims

Mariner Corp. & Shannon Corp. v. Dardent Corp. & Dreyfus Corp.

Mariner Corporation, a Delaware corporation with its principal place of business in Texas, and Shannon Corporation, another Delaware corporation with its principal place of business in California, sued Dardent Corporation, a Michigan corporation with its principal place of business in Pennsylvania, and Dreyfuss Corporation, a Pennsylvania corporation with its principal place of business in New Jersey. The case was filed in a United States District Court in Pennsylvania on a state breach of contract claim alleging damages in excess of $6,000,000. Dreyfuss Corporation then filed a third party complaint alleging that General Corporation, a New Mexico corporation with its principal place of business in California owed to Dreyfuss any amounts Dreyfuss is found to owe to Mariner Corporation.

Questions

1. Is this a proper third party claim? Why or why not?

2. Suppose, instead, that as a result of a counterclaim by one of the defendants, Shannon Corporation sought to bring a third party complaint against General Corporation for any amounts Shannon might owe to the counterclaiming defendant. Would that be a proper third party claim? Why or why not?

Pleading Third Party Claims

Keating v. Castle and Tennent v. Albert Transport, Inc.

Frederick R. Keating is a citizen of Mississippi. Robert Castle and Jonathan Tennent are both citizens of Oklahoma. Keating filed an action in an appropriate federal district court alleging violations of federal racketeering laws against both Castle and Tennent alleging that these two, doing business as Angle Investing used the mail and interstate telephone communications to obtain Keating's $600,0000 investment in DLI Concepts, a holding company that was alleged to be purchasing the stock of Albert Transport, Inc., an over the road trucking company and corporate citizen of Delaware. In fact, the complaint alleged that the money obtained from Keating was used to pay Castle and Tennent inflated salaries and not provide the basis of an investment in Albert Transport. As a result of the diversion of funds, Keating alleged that Albert Transport suffered severe financial reversals and when the sale was ultimately consummated, Keating's shares in this acquisition were not worth what he had been led to believe. In response to the action, Castle and Tennent both filed third party complaints against Albert Trucking seeking contribution. Those third party complaints both said: "Castle and Tennent are entitled to indemnity and contribution from Albert Trucking in the event of a judgment against either or both of them."

Question

Albert Trucking moves to dismiss the Third Party Complaint filed against it by Tennent, alleging a failure to comply with Rule 8(a)'s requirement of a "short and plain" statement of the claim. What result? Why?

Joinder of Parties--Necessary/Indispensable Parties

Evans v. Alpha Sigma Nu Sorority of Sisters, Inc.

Alpha Sigma Nu Corporation is a corporate citizen of Ohio and is the national leadership organization from which local Alpha Sigma Nu sorority chapters take their charter. The Alpha Sigma Nu Sorority of Sisters, Inc., is a Kentucky not-for profit corporation the sole purpose of which was to purchase property to be used by the local sorority chapter at Western Kentucky Wesleyan University. The officers and directors of Sorority of Sisters are all adult alumnae of the local chapter. The Sorority of Sisters purchased a tract of land on the Kentucky border with Illinois and allowed the Western Kentucky Wesleyan chapter to use the land to hold sorority social events. Rhonda Evans is a citizen of Illinois who resides in Illinois on land immediately adjacent to the Sorority of Sisters tract. After numerous parties and other social events held by the local chapter involved unruly crowds of students who were bussed to the property from the university, Rhonda Evans complained about the noise and behavior of the students to the Sorority of Sisters and to the national corporation, which stood as a guarantor on the mortgage to the property. After those complaints went unheeded, Rhonda Evans filed suit alleging that the use of the property constituted a nuisance and rendered her property, valued at $400,000 valueless. The suit was filed in the federal court in Kentucky against Alpha Sigma Nu Sorority of Sisters, Inc.

Questions

1. The Sorority of Sisters moved to dismiss the complaint for failure to join an y of the students who were actually causing the disturbance as necessary parties. Is that motion proper? Why or why not?

2. Assuming a proper motion before the court, what analysis should the court conduct?

3. Are the students necessary/indispensable? Why or why not?

Bell v. Board of Trustees of Dartmouth College

Coleridge Bell is a citizen of Mississippi and an alumnus of Dartmouth College. Under an 1891 understanding between Dartmouth and its alumni, the College alumni effectively choose a certain number of the College's trustees; the Dartmouth College Alumni Association, an organization formed after the 1891 agreement and comprising all Dartmouth alumni, conducts an election if there is any contest among nominees. Prior to last year, this process was used to fill both a trustee's initial term and any subsequent terms.

Last year, Dartmouth's Board of Trustees, the incorporated governing body of Dartmouth College and a corporate citizen of New Hampshire, and the Alumni Association modified this arrangement in one respect: under this new agreement, the Board of Trustees has the power to reseat a trustee, originally chosen by the alumni, for an additional term without obtaining the alumni's further approval. The Alumni Association, also a corporate citizen of New Hampshire, amended its constitution to reflect this change.

Coleridge Bell and several of his alumni friends were furious to lose their right to determine if members of the Board of Trustees should be reseated. They filed suit in the United States District Court for the

District of New Hampshire against the Board of Trustees of Dartmouth College alleging that the 1891 understanding was a contract between the College and the individual members of the alumni association and that the Trustees were in breach of that agreement with the new arrangement with the Alumni Association.

The Board of Trustees has moved to dismiss the matter in the absence of what it claims is a necessary party, the Alumni Association.

Questions

1. What is your analysis of whether the Alumni Association is a necessary party?

2. If the Alumni Association is a necessary party, is there any reason the Association cannot be joined to a proceeding in the District Court in New Hampshire under Rule 19?

3. Why does the Board of Trustees seek to dismiss the action if the Alumni Association could be joined?

In re Cherokee Nation

Prior to the settlement in America by Europeans, the Cherokee and Delaware Indians resided in the eastern portion of what is now the United States. In the 1830s, the federal government removed many Cherokee from the eastern United States to Indian Territory where they eventually settled in what is now northeastern Oklahoma The Delaware were removed west as well. Following the Civil War, pressure from railroads and white settlers forced removal of Indians from Kansas and other western areas. In an 1866 Treaty, the Cherokee Nation agreed to accept groups of resettled Indians in its territory under certain conditions and, as a result, one of five branches of the Delaware tribe, known as the Cherokee Delaware, resettled in Cherokee territory.

The terms and conditions on which the Delaware Tribe settled on Cherokee land are contained in an 1867 agreement that provided for the settlement of Delaware in Cherokee Nation territory in accordance with Article 15 of the 1866 Treaty. Article 15 of the Treaty provided that Indian groups could settle in Cherokee Nation territory east of the 96° of longitude by either: (1) becoming members of the Cherokee Nation, with the same rights and immunities, and the same participation in the national funds, as native Cherokees, with their children born thereafter being regarded as native Cherokee in all respects; or (2) maintaining their tribal laws, customs, and usages, and receiving a district of land set off for their use.

Since the time of the 1867 Agreement, there has been some uncertainty as to the Delaware Tribe's political status. After several court decisions, the United States Department of the Interior issued a letter to the Chairman of the Cherokee Delaware Business Committee notifying him that the Bureau was withdrawing its prior approval of the Committee's By-Laws because the Committee was "not capable of adequately protecting the interests of the Cherokee Delaware people," and because the Committee had failed to meet a deadline the Bureau previously set for forming a Committee to draft adequate By-Laws. Following the time required under federal administrative law, the Assistant Secretary of Indian Affairs, U.S. Department of Interior, issued a Notice of Final Agency Action acknowledging the Delaware Tribe of Indians' status as a tribe independent of the Cherokee Nation. In so doing, the Department recognized that the Delaware Tribe is a "separate sovereign," "with the same legal rights and responsibilities as other tribes," and "eligible for funding and services from the Bureau of Indian Affairs by virtue of its status as an Indian tribe."

The Cherokee Nation filed suit in the correct Federal Court alleging that the actions of the Department were erroneous because the Cherokee Delaware tribe was not an independent sovereign because it was instead a member of the Cherokee Nation.

Questions

1. Is the Cherokee Delaware tribe a "necessary" party to this litigation?

2. Is the Cherokee Delaware tribe an "Indispensable" party to this litigation?

3. What standards should the court using in answering these questions?

Joinder of Parties– Intervention

Planned Parenthood v. State of Missouri

For many years, the Missouri Legislature annually enacted a program where the Missouri Department of Health financed family planning services for low income men and women. Prior to five years ago, the legislature's appropriation restricted program recipients from using family planning funds to perform or promote abortions. The legislation did not, however, prohibit entities that provided abortion services from participating in the program.

Planned Parenthood of Central Missouri, a Missouri corporation, provides family planning and related medical services to residents of twenty-six Missouri counties. Planned Parenthood performs abortions at two of their nine clinics located in Missouri. In addition, Planned Parenthood engages in public advocacy to protect safe and legal access to abortion services for women.

Five years ago, the Missouri Legislature enacted House Bill 10 which according to the Department's interpretation expressly excluded Planned Parenthood from family planning funds because it is an entity that provides abortion services.

Planned Parenthood argued that the legislation unconstitutionally excluded it from eligibility because it was the only entity excluded after receiving funding in previous years and the only entity that provided abortions. As a result, Planned Parenthood filed suit in the United States District Court for the Western District of Missouri. That suit, among other things, contended that the Department relied on an unconstitutional statute in excluding it from funding. Following a hearing, the district court granted Planned Parenthood's motions for an injunction. The court enjoined the Department from excluding Planned Parenthood from the remaining family planning funds because Planned Parenthood provides abortions and engages in public advocacy of safe and legal abortions. The Missouri Attorney General, who represented the Department, did not appeal the district court order.

The following year, while the injunction was in effect, and apparently in response to it, the Missouri Legislature enacted H.B. 20 which provided family planning funding in three tiers. In the first tier, the Department could pay or grant family planning funds to public, quasi-public and private family planning organizations that did not provide or promote abortions. If a court determined any portion of the first tier to be unconstitutional, then the Department was required to abandon first tier funding and move to the second tier. The second tier provided that the Department could grant family planning funds to public and quasi-public family planning organizations but not to private organizations. Again, organizations could not use funds to promote or encourage abortions. If a court invalidated both the first and second tiers, the Department was required to abandon first and second tier funding and move to a third tier. Under the third tier, only public organizations could receive family planning funds.

Prior to the enactment of H.B. 20, the Missouri Attorney General expressed opposition to the legislation, indicating it was an attempt to exclude Planned Parenthood, but despite that opposition, the Governor signed H.B. 20 into law. In a statement accompanying the signing, the Governor acknowledged his obligation to uphold the law stating Planned Parenthood would not receive funds. However, the Governor also stated his intent to direct the Missouri Attorney General to seek clarification from the district court about the applicability of the district court's injunction.

Thereafter, the Missouri Attorney General filed a motion to clarify and suggestions in support with the explanation that the Department and the Missouri Attorney General desired to comply with the district court's permanent injunction. In response to this motion, the district court held a brief telephone conference with counsel to hear arguments on the Missouri Attorney General's motion. Later that same day, the district court declared H.B. 20 unconstitutional. The Missouri Attorney General did not appeal the district court's ruling.

At that point, ten legislators, Missouri senators and representatives who voted for H.B. 20, sought intervention on the side of the Department to defend the constitutionality of H.B. 20. One of those legislators was Harriet Oliver. The ten legislators contended that the Missouri Attorney General did not offer any arguments in support of the constitutionality of H.B. 20. The ten legislators also contended the Missouri Attorney General failed to attempt to explain the severability of the three-tiered system. The ten legislators' motion to intervene sought leave to intervene as of right, pursuant to section 24(a) of the Federal Rules of Civil Procedure or for leave to intervene permissibly pursuant to section 24(b) of the Federal Rules of Civil Procedure.

Questions

1. How should the court rule on the Rule 24(a) motion? Why?
2. How should the court rule on the Rule 24(b) motion? Why?

Joinder of Parties--Interpleader

In re Greyhound Bus Accident

Ellis Clark, a citizen of Oklahoma, was the negligent driver of a Greyhound bus which collided with a truck driven by Kenneth Glasgow. Greyhound Bus Co. is a corporate citizen of New York. In the accident, 38 people on the Greyhound bus were injured or killed, and both Clark and Glasgow were also seriously injured. Some, but not all, of the 39 victims were citizens of Oklahoma. Farmers and Bankers Mutual Insurance Co., an Illinois corporation has written an automobile insurance policy for Ellis Clark. That policy provides for coverage for up to $10,000 per person with a limit of $20,000 per accident. Farmers and Bankers is aware that each of the 39 victims of Clark's negligence is planning on filing suit against Clark and Greyhound. Because it is limited to a maximum of $20,000 coverage in the case, Farmers and Bankers has asked you if it can file some sort of action to pay its $20,000 into court and be dismissed from the case.

Question

Discuss the relative merits of either a "Rule" or "Statutory" interpleader action. What assumptions will you have to make for either action? Why?

Joinder of Parties--Substitution

Santiago v. Valerie Hobson, d/b/a Ren Farms

Angel Santiago, a citizen of Mexico, is a resident alien migrant farm worker who, along with others, was employed at Ren Farms, an unincorporated apple orchard being operated by Valerie Hobson. Hobson was a citizen of and the orchard was located in the State of Washington. Angel Santiago and some ten other migrant farm workers filed a lawsuit in the federal district court in Washington state alleging that Hobson, doing business as Ren Farms, had violated several sections of the federal Migrant and Seasonal Agricultural Workers Protection Act [AWPA], 29 U.S.C. §1801 et seq. The violations related, according to the Complaint, to the wrongful discharge of Santiago and his colleagues. After a jury trial, Santiago and the other migrant workers were awarded a judgment in excess of $200,000. Following that judgment, Valerie Hobson signed quit claim deeds transferring the Ren Farms orchard to AppleRen, Inc., a Washington corporation. Valerie Hobson is a 1% owner of AppleRen, Inc. and her two sons, Arnold and William, equally own the balance. Since the transfer of ownership, Arnold Hobson has taken a more active role in the management of the orchard, but Valerie has also undertaken some management responsibility.

Question

When Angel Santiago and his colleagues sought to execute on their judgment against Valerie Hobson, doing business as Ren Farms, they learned for the first time of the transfer of ownership. Because Valerie Hobson has insufficient other assets to pay the judgment, Santiago's counsel would like to substitute AppleRen, Inc. as a defendant in the action for Valerie Hobson, doing business as Ren Farm. How should this be accomplished?

Class Actions--Generally

Preynore v. Cousin Earl's Pizza, Inc.

Anne Preynore is a citizen of New Mexico. Cousin Earl's Pizza, Inc. is a corporate citizen of Delaware and does business in about forty-five states. Cousin Earl's sells pizza from small store-front stores both through carry-out and home delivery.

In a recent Sunday newspaper campaign around the country, Cousin Earl's ran the following advertisement:

Absolutely FREE Garlic Stix

This coupon entitles you to absolutely FREE Garlic Stix with the purchase of ONE large One Topping Cousin Earl's Pizza for $9.99* Good until end of this month only.

(*Large One Topping Pizza without Garlic Stix $8.99)

Anne Preynore purchased several large one topping Earl's pizzas for her family in order to get her "free" Garlic Stix until her ten year old daughter said to her one evening: "You know, Mom, you're paying $1.00 for your free Garlic Stix." When Anne read the advertisement carefully, she was incensed and went to her lawyer, who immediately began a nationwide Class Action against Cousin Earl's.

Questions

1. What is Anne's damage? Is there a federal question here? Assuming this is a diversity case and assuming that class certification could be granted, how can this case ever find its way into the federal court?

2. Why would a lawyer take this case?

3. Assuming that a lawyer is able to advertise on national television and attract 200,000 plaintiffs, what remedy is each of them likely to get from this case?

4. How does any of this advance any of the goals of litigation that you have studied in this course?

Beban, et als. v. National Collegiate Athletic Association

The National Collegiate Athletic Association is a voluntary, nonprofit, standard-setting association that promulgates the rules of competition for and operates annual national championships in 22 sports across three divisions. Over 1,200 educational institutions, athletic conferences, and related organizations are members of the NCAA. The NCAA regulates intercollegiate athletics in a number of ways, including prescribing rules of play, defining the length of seasons, imposing recruiting constraints, maintaining athletics records, defining eligibility parameters for players, delineating allowable coaching structures, and imposing sanctions when its rules are broken.

One such rule is NCAA Bylaw 15.5.5, which imposes annual limits on the number of football scholarships that a member school may award. For the NCAA's largest football schools, Division I-A schools, an institution is limited to 85 players who receive financial aid. These players are called "counters." Additionally, many football teams carry additional players, called "walk-ons." There is no limit on the size of Division 1-A football team rosters, although the average is about 115 players during the football season. The NCAA further limits teams however, to a total of 105 players who are eligible to participate in pre-football-season practices. Thus, if a university had its full compliment of 85 scholarship players, and carried an in-season roster of 115, there would be 20 players who would be eligible to participate in pre-season training with the team and 10 additional players who could not. At any time, a school could give a "walk-on" player a scholarship and that player would then become a "counter" towards the school's 85 scholarships. Marcus Beban, George White, Charles Rogers, Steve Dawkins and Pete Allen are all walk-on football players who played at Division I-A football schools. They each play at a different school in a different state. Each of them was one of the 20 players who was not on scholarship but who was eligible to participate in pre-season practices with their college's teams. It is these players who, traditionally, receive any scholarships should one of the 85 "counter" positions become available.

Marcus Beban, George White, Charles Rogers, Steve Dawkins and Pete Allen have filed suit seeking injunctive relief invalidating Bylaw 15.5.5 (or any similar rule restricting the number of "counters"), as well as money damages (to be trebled according to federal statute), costs, and fees. The Court denied the NCAA's Rule 12(c) motion for judgment on the pleadings. The plaintiffs now seek to have the action certified as a Class Action.

Questions

1. The facts do not tell you where this action was filed. For all of these problems, assume the action is filed in federal court, how is their subject matter jurisdiction?

2. What are appropriate venue locations?

3. Are each of the requirements under Rule 23(a) met? How?

Rule 23(b)(1) Class Actions

In re Dodger Industries Retirement Investment Plan

Dodger Industries, Inc. is a Delaware corporation which provides real estate investment advice to consumers. It has offices and employees nationwide. For its employees, Dodger Industries maintains the Dodger Industries Retirement Investment Plan, a plan set up to comply with federal employment laws. The Plan allows employees to invest their earnings through tax deferred contributions. Dodger Industries also contributes to the Plan through matching contributions. There is an additional employee stock option plan which is also funded by the company through contributions that are made primarily in company stock into the Dodger Industries Fund.

Recently, employees and former employees who participated in and continue to participate in the Dodger Industries Retirement Investment Plan and stock option plan filed a federal court action in the nature of a class action seeking to recover alleged losses of retirement savings of employees and former employees. There are approximately 7,000 employees and former employees affected by the issues raised here. Approximately 1,000 of these 7,000 employees profited from participation in the plan while the other 6,000 all lost money. The employees and former employees named as defendants Dodger Industries and the named directors, officers and/or employees of Dodger Industries (the "Individual Defendants") (collectively, "Defendants"), all of whom it was alleged were fiduciaries of the Plan, as defined by federal law. The essence of the complaint is that Dodger Industries stock was inflated during the proposed Class Period by the acts of Dodger Industries and its directors, and that while it was inflated the fiduciaries of the Plan imprudently permitted Plan participants to continue to invest in Dodger Industries stock.

Plaintiffs allege that all of the defendants breached numerous fiduciary duties existing under federal law related to investigation of investment possibilities with the plan, monitoring of plan profitability, disclosure to plaintiffs, and self dealing. Plaintiffs also allege that defendants breached duties of loyalty by being involved in numerous conflicts of interest that impacted the profitability of the plan.

Questions

As clerk to the federal district court judge to whom this case is assigned to determine if this class should be certified, conduct an analysis of this case's suitability for class action status. Among the various arguments of counsel, you should consider the following:

1. Defendants indicate that the class cannot be certified because

of conflict of interest in that 1,000 of the plaintiffs actually profited.

    2. Plaintiffs argue that the class should be certified as a Rule 23(b)(1)(A) class because of the risk of inconsistent or varying results for individual class members.

    3. Plaintiffs argue that the class should be certified as a Rule 23(b)(1)(B) class because litigation regarding one of the plaintiffs would be dispositive as to the claims of others.

    4. Defendants claim that each individual has a separate claim and that consideration of these individual losses would undermine class management.

Rule 23(b)(2) Class Actions

In re Crown Insurance Company

    Crown Insurance, Inc. is a Delaware corporation and a nationwide issuer of automobile and other liability insurance. At one time, Crown marketed its insurance through company-employed agents. In what it termed as "cost containment" several years ago, Crown decided to replace all of its employee insurance agents with independent contractors. Under federal law, before it could replace these employees, Crown needed to provide the soon-to-be former employees with a severance package.

    Arte Lampkin, Serena Williamson, Benoit Anderson, and Renee Morton were all employee agents of Crown and were the members of the Executive Committee of the Crown Agents' Association, an unincorporated trade group of agents. Lampkin, Williamson, Anderson and Morton all claimed that Crown harassed them, and other agents, in violation of federal law so that they would quit before they could take advantage of the severance benefits . The company, it is claimed, harassed the agents by extending office hours, imposing burdensome reporting requirements, reducing or eliminating reimbursement for office expenses, and setting unrealistic sales quotas. As a result of the campaign of harassment, 176 national agents quit outright and 1,106 others quit as employees but became independent contractors. Lampkin, Williamson, Anderson, and Morton have filed a class action in the appropriate United States District Court against Crown Insurance. They claim that the class seeks a judgment declaring that the members are entitled to the benefits they would have received under Crown's federally required retirement plan had they been terminated in Crown's "cost containment" maneuver rather than quitting. They also seek injunctive relief preventing Crown from any conduct that would cause dissipation of any financial benefits over which Crown maintains control. The basis for this relief is the fact that Crown controls the total amount of money set aside for retirement and other benefits for retired or discharged employees.

Questions

Lampkin, Williamson, Anderson, and Morton seek to certify this action as a Rule 23(b)(2) class. Crown opposes this indicating that if the class is certified, it should be certified as a Rule 23(b)(3) class.
1. What is the difference?
2. Why does the difference matter?
3. How should the court decide.

Class Actions–Burden of Proof under CAFA

Adelman v. Express Shipping Services, Inc.

Monroe Adelman, a citizen of Wyoming, filed suit against Express Shipping Services, Inc. (ESS), a corporation with its principal place of business in Wyoming. Adelman's suit was filed in Wyoming state court and alleged that he represented himself and all persons that ESS employed in Wyoming as local package delivery drivers who were or are improperly classified as "independent contractors." In his complaint, Adelman alleged that federal jurisdiction was lacking "because the defendant and greater than two-thirds of the members of the plaintiff class, if not all of the members of the plaintiff class, are citizens of Wyoming." ESS filed a notice of removal claiming diversity jurisdiction pursuant to the Class Action Certification Act, § 1332(d), stating that "[u]pon information and belief, some of the proposed class members are not residents of Wyoming." After removal, Adelman moved for remand, alleging that there were insufficient class members to create diversity. In response, ESS provided affidavits from employees showing that at least 12 members of the proposed class were not citizens of Wyoming.

Questions

1. Adelman alleges that ESS must prove there are sufficient citizens of different states to justify diversity while ESS alleges that once it shows that at least one class member is from a state other than Wyoming, Adelman bears the burden of proving that the exception contained in §1332(d)(4)(A) is applicable. Who is right? Why?
2. What difference does it make who has to prove what?

Class Actions–Notice

Weiss v. New Horizons Mutual Insurance Co.

Aaron and Adele Weiss are citizens of Texas. New Horizons Insurance Co. is a Delaware corporation that writes automobile, property and casualty insurance on a nationwide basis. The Weiss' purchased automobile insurance from New Horizons. One of the provisions of that policy promises to "pay loss in money or repair or replace damaged or stolen property." Under the company's guidelines for its adjusters, New Horizons instructs adjusters to separate cars by whether they are less then three years old. For vehicles in the latest three model years, adjusters are instructed to specify Original Equipment Manufacturer ("OEM") replacement parts for repairs. These are parts made by the original manufacturer of the automobile. When writing estimates for vehicles of an earlier model year, adjusters are encouraged to specify the use of non-OEM crash parts or salvage OEM parts. These are parts made by outside companies without access to the design of the original part.

Following a loss to their four year old car, the Weiss' learned of New Horizons instructions to its adjusters and thereafter filed a lawsuit in a proper federal court alleging that New Horizons breached its contracts with policyholders to restore their vehicles to pre-loss condition by devising and implementing a practice that results in payment of claims based on (1) the systematic specification of "inferior" non-OEM crash parts for repairs and (2) the systematic omission of specific "necessary" repairs from estimates. The Weiss' brought the action on behalf of themselves and "all others nationwide" who were insured by New Horizons, made a claim for vehicle repairs pursuant to their policy, and received payment based on an estimate prepared or approved by New Horizons that included non-OEM crash parts and/or did not include specified "necessary" repairs.

Question

Assume the court is prepared to certify the action as a Class Action pursuant to Rule 23(b)(3). How should notice be provided?

Class Action Settlements

In re "NFL Sunday Ticket"

Some number of years ago, a group of 1.8 million plaintiffs filed a federal class action against the National Football League alleging that a satellite television package of National Football League football games known as "NFL Sunday Ticket" violated federal antitrust laws. After extensive litigation, the case settled, and the plaintiff class received $7.5 million in cash (in addition to attorneys' fees, costs and costs of administration) plus the benefit of certain injunctive relief. Following that settlement, disbursement was made from the fund to cla ss members. Individual class members were required to make a claim and, upon approval, a check was issued to the class member for the appropriate amount. In addition to those claims that were paid and for which checks were cashed, there were approximately $436,000 in claims that were made against the fund, but for which the checks issued to the claimants were never cashed. Those funds remain and the plaintiffs and defendants have jointly moved to have the court disburse those funds. Plaintiffs and defendants differ, however, on what should happen to the funds. Plaintiffs propose that the unclaimed funds be allocated as follows: (1) $50,000 to provide the class with a reminder publication notice of the alternative programming ("NFL Sunday Ticket Pay-Per-Day"), (2) $100,000 to a law school clinical education program and (3) the remainder, approximately $286,000, toward the establishment of a high school scholarship program to assist graduating students who have excelled academically but are unable to afford college preparatory, private or parochial high schools. The defendants propose that the funds be distributed to the NFL Youth Education Town Centers ("NFL YET Centers"), which are located in every city that has hosted a Super Bowl for the last twelve years. The NFL YET Centers, operated by the Boys and Girls Clubs of America, but funded in part by the NFL, have a goal of enhancing educational and vocational opportunities for children in low-income neighborhoods, including providing tutorial, counseling and mentoring services, as well as computers and other technological tools. The facilities generally include libraries, classrooms, technology labs and fitness centers.

Questions

1. How can the court do either of the proposals? That is, what gives the court the right to take money allocated for one purpose and turn it into something else?

2. What should the court do? Why?

CHAPTER 7

DISCOVERY

Mandatory Disclosures and Discovery Conference

Kendall v. Brown

George Kendall, a citizen of Maine, was visiting his cousin in Massachusetts. Kendall had driven to Massachusetts with his German Shepherd dog, Alfie. Leonard Brown, a citizen of Massachusetts, was the neighbor of Kendall's cousin.. One afternoon, while Kendall was enjoying his cousin's swimming pool, he heard a commotion in the adjoining yard. When he arrived, he saw Alfie engaged in a fight with George Brown's mixed breed dog, Rufus. To his chagrin, Brown had a stick about four feet long and was beating both of the dogs. Brown was apparently trying to get the dogs to stop fighting because he kept yelling "Stop it! Right now!" Originally about sixteen feet away from the dispute, Kendall moved towards the dogs at the same time as the dogs began moving towards him. Leonard Brown, who was facing away from Kendall, kept hitting the dogs with the stick but also kept moving backwards as the dogs moved toward Kendall. As Brown approached with his back towards Kendall, Brown raised the stick over his shoulder and hit George Kendall in the eye inflicting severe injuries. The police were called, the dogs were subdued and Kendall was taken to the hospital. Kendall was treated in the hospital, was disabled from his regular job as an over-the-road truck driver for a substantial period and is still receiving treatment. In addition, both Kendall and Brown were charged in criminal court with allowing their dogs to run loose.

George Kendall sued Leonard Brown in the United States District Court for the District of Massachusetts. Brown's attorneys filed an answer.

Questions

1. You represent George Kendall. Prepare a list of the items you would expect to receive from Brown's lawyers under Rule 26(a)(1).

2. You represent Leonard Brown. Prepare a list of the items you would expect to receive from Brown's lawyers under Rule 26(a)(1).

3. As attorney for George Kendall, state the information you think it will be necessary for you to obtain during discovery and what you consider to be the preferred discovery method for obtaining that information.

4. As attorney for either Kendall or Brown, state as specifically as possible what you expect will be discussed at the Discovery Conference under Rule 26(f).

Judicial Control over Discovery– Protective Orders

Smithton v. Buchner

Charles Smithton, a citizen of Michigan, was a probationary police officer in the city of East Lansing. He was fired on grounds that he sexually harassed female probationary colleagues at the police training academy. Smithton sued Jolina Buchner, the superintendent of police of the City of East Lansing. Smithton claimed that firing him prevented him from obtaining other employment as a police officer, which, in turn, curtailed his liberty of employment without due process of law. As a probationary police officer, Smithton was denied a hearing before he was fired, a hearing that would automatically be granted to regular employees of the police department. Smith argued that these activities constituted a violation of his due process rights and were therefore a violation of his federal Constitutional rights. The facts are unusual because there is no evidence that Commissioner Buchner or any member of the police department actually disclosed to anyone the grounds of Smithton's discharge. Rather, Smithton argues that this failure makes no difference to his employability because no police department will hire him without asking him why he was fired by the Department. If he answers truthfully, he will reveal the ground of the termination as effectively as (actually more effectively than) if the Department had taken out a full-page ad in every newspaper in the nation announcing his termination for sexually harassing female probationary officers at the police training academy.

Following an answer by Buchner, Smithton sought to take the deposition of Buchner. On motion by Buchner's counsel under Rule 26(c), the trial judge entered a protective order and, in doing so, refused to permit Smithton to depose Buchner until the plaintiff submitted written interrogatories the answers to which would indicate whether deposing the defendant would serve a useful purpose. The judge was influenced in following this course of action by the fact that the superintendent of the East Lansing police is a busy official who should not be taken away from her work to spend hours or days answering lawyers' questions unless there was a real need.

Question

Discuss the judge's action.

Discovery Relevance

Condit v. Dunne

Gary Condit is a former United States Congressman for the 18th District of California and is a citizen of California. Dominick Dunne is a citizen of New York and is a special correspondent for *Vanity Fair* magazine, an author, and a television commentator.

Chandra Levy was a 24-year old employee of the United States Bureau of Prisons who disappeared from her downtown Washington, D.C. apartment. Sometime after the disappearance, Gary Condit publicly acknowledged that he and Ms. Levy were friends. As law enforcement investigated Ms. Levy's disappearance, a media frenzy ensued which focused in no small part on speculation about the relationship between plaintiff and Ms. Levy.

During this investigative stage, Dominick Dunne appeared on *The Laura Ingraham Show,* a nationally syndicated radio talk show. After being introduced as having followed the Levy case, Mr. Dunne indicated that he had spoken with a person from Salinas, California, who did extensive traveling in the Middle East. This person had met another in the Mideast who told Dunne's source that Gary Condit was often a guest at some of the Middle Eastern embassies in Washington, and that Condit had let it be known that he was in a relationship with a woman. Condit claimed the relationship was over, but that the woman "was a clinger." He couldn't get rid of her. And he had made promises to her that he couldn't keep and apparently she knew things about him and threatened to go public. And at one point he said the woman was driving him crazy, or words to that effect. Dunne said that his source indicated that the person from the Middle East indicated that it's very easy for them to make people disappear. He said that she was put in a limousine, and the Mideast source said that he saw her being put on a plane, one of these big commercial-sized private planes that the Arabs have, rich princes, and those people.... And he said, let me put it this way. She wasn't walking.

About a year after her disappearance, Ms. Levy's remains were found in Rock Creek Park in Washington, D.C. Shortly after Ms. Levy's remains were recovered, Dominic Dunne was interviewed separately by reporters for the *Boston Herald* and *USA Today*. The "Inside Track" column of the *Boston Herald* subsequently reported, under the title "Condit get a Dunne-ing," that Dunne "still believes Washington intern Chandra Levy was the victim of foul play and the discovery of her body doesn't let Congressman Gary Condit off the hook." *USA Today,* in its print version and on its website, subsequently published a story titled "Dunne's trail leads to the elite of murders." *USA Today* quotes Dunne as saying "I don't think [Condit] killed her. I think he could have known it was going to happen."

Gary Condit filed a defamation action against Dunne in the United States District Court for the Southern District of New York. Condit alleged that Dunne's statements constituted slander *per se* because they charge Condit with serious crimes involving moral turpitude. Further, plaintiff alleged that Dunne's statements directly and proximately led the public to believe Condit was guilty of criminal involvement in the disappearance and death of Ms. Levy, and caused Condit's reputation to suffer accordingly. Condit alleged he suffered stress, emotional distress and mental pain and suffering, adverse physical consequences, public hatred, contempt and ridicule, all as a direct and proximate result of Dunne's statements. Finally, plaintiff pleaded special damages claiming he suffered permanent impairment to his ability to obtain gainful employment from third parties. Condit sought one million dollars ($1,000,000) in compensatory damages, ten million dollars ($10,000,000) in punitive damages, plus costs and attorneys' fees.

Following the complaint and answer, the parties began discovery. In his deposition, plaintiff Condit refused to answer certain questions. Specifically, plaintiff Condit refused to answer questions relating to: 1) his sexual relationships; and 2) his financial status.

Question

Discuss the discovery relevance of the two series of questions Mr. Condit refused to answer.

Discovery Privilege

Horton v. Prescott International, Inc.

Margaret Horton, a citizen of Ohio, filed a complaint in the Federal District Court for the Western District of Pennsylvania against her employer, Prescott International Inc., a Pennsylvania corporation under a Pennsylvania Human Rights statute. Horton alleged sex discrimination and sexual harassment during her employment at Prescott. Horton's complaint sought damages for loss of income, and "emotional distress, humiliation, inconvenience, and loss of enjoyment of life."

Attorneys for Prescott then propounded discovery requests to Horton, including interrogatories and requests for production of documents. Prescott's Interrogatory 1 asked Horton if she claimed, as a result of the matters alleged in her Complaint, that she had been "treated or attended by any hospitals, doctors, nurses, psychologists, counselors, or others in the healing arts. If your answer is 'yes,' state as to each hospital, doctor, nurse, psychologist, counselor, or others in the healing arts the name, address and telephone number; the dates of all such treatments or attendances." Horton replied "No" to this interrogatory.

Interrogatory 2 asked Horton to "identify each item of damage you claim you sustained as a result of the conduct of defendant [Prescott] as alleged in the Complaint; and further state the dollar amount you are claiming for each item of damage; and the manner in which you have calculated the dollar amount of each such item of damages." Horton replied that she was claiming "Emotional Distress, Embarrassment, and Humiliation-Plaintiff is, at this time, seeking only 'garden variety' emotional distress damages."

Interrogatory 12, to which Horton objected, asked Horton to "State whether you have *ever* consulted or been treated by a psychiatrist, psychologist, counselor or other health care practitioner for mental distress, emotional suffering or any other mental or emotional condition. If your answer is 'yes,' state as to each hospital, doctor, nurse, psychologist, counselor, or others in the healing arts the name, address and telephone number; the dates of all such treatments or attendances." Horton's objection to Interrogatory 12 was based, in part, on the physician-patient privilege and the fact that the interrogatory was not limited in scope and time.

Prescott's request for production of documents number 13 asked Horton to produce "all medical records, reports, charts or notations of any kind describing or indicating plaintiffs (sic) physical or mental condition prepared by any physician, therapist, or any other person having occasion to treat, examine or care for plaintiff as requested in

Interrogatory Number 1, and additionally, plaintiff is requested to execute the medical records release attached hereto to enable defendant [Prescott] to acquire such documents." Horton objected to the request, in part, by asserting the physician-patient privilege and that the request was not limited in time.

Additionally, Horton refused to execute the medical record release attached to request for production of documents number 13. The attached release authorized Prescott's attorneys to "inspect and copy all office, medical and hospital records, reports and other medical documents" in the possession of the recipient "and relating to illnesses of or injuries, examinations, treatment or confinement of the patient." The authorization included "records of all examinations, treatments and tests, including in-patient, out-patient and emergency room, whether for diagnostic or prognostic purposes, consultation reports, correspondence, x-rays, nurses notes, bills, doctors notes, photographs, videotapes, MRIs, and CT scans, workers' compensation records, psychologists notes and mental health records." The authorization left a blank line after the "TO:" designation and was not, itself, limited to mental health care providers.

After Horton's objections to its discovery, Prescott sought an order to compel discovery from the trial judge.

Question

Attorneys for Prescott allege that "[b]y pleading for emotional distress damages, [Horton] place[d] her mental and emotional condition at issue and, thus, ma[de] her mental health treatment history discoverable." Do you agree? Why or why not?

Blocker v. Remington Oil, Inc.

Francis and Evelyn Blocker, citizens of Montana, filed suit against Remington Oil, Inc., an Idaho corporation in the United States District Court for the District of Montana alleging that Remington intentionally dumped diesel oil and toxic solvents on the Blocker's land, resulting in contamination of the land, and for Remington Oil's intentional failure to contain and remediate this damage. The Blockers' complaint sought recovery for nuisance, negligence, strict liability, trespass, wrongful occupation, violations of the Montana Constitution, unjust enrichment, and misconduct warranting punitive damages. Shortly after the pleadings closed, the Blockers served their first set of document requests pursuant to Rule 34. This was followed by several other requests for production of documents. As to each, Remington filed a response with the Blockers indicating the documents were "privileged."

After three such instances, the Blockers filed a motion to compel and for sanctions.

Questions

1. When Remington sought to claim that documents sought under Rule 34 were privileged, is there anything wrong with their statement: "These documents are privileged?" What?

2. If privilege is improperly raised, has the privilege been waived? Why or why not?

Discovery Work Product

Lockwood v. Lawrence Partnership, Ltd.

In February, two years ago, the tugboat David Lawrence sank while engaged in towing a container ship in the Port of New Orleans. Five of the nine crew members of the David Lawrence were drowned. Three days later, the owners of the David Lawrence and the Prime Vessel Insurance Company, which wrote the insurance on the vessel, employed Arnold Anson of the law firm of Anson & Cappel to defend both the tugboat owners against potential suits by representatives of the deceased crew members and to sue the owners of the container ship for damages to the tug.

A public hearing before the United States Steamboat Inspectors was held the following month. The four survivors of the David Lawrence were examined. This testimony was recorded and made available to all interested parties. Shortly thereafter, Arnold Anson, on behalf of his clients, privately interviewed the survivors and took statements from them with an eye toward the anticipated litigation; the survivors signed these statements roughly seven weeks following the accident. Anson also interviewed other persons believed to have some information relating to the accident and in some cases he made memoranda of what they told him. At the time when Anson secured the statements of the survivors, representatives of two of the deceased crew members had been in communication with him. Ultimately claims were presented by representatives of all five of the deceased; four of the claims, however, were settled without litigation. The fifth claimant, Sergant Lockwood, brought suit in the United States District Court for the District of Louisiana under federal legislation known as the Jones Act. Lockwood sued the Lawrence Partnership, Ltd., the owners of the David Lawrence, individually and as partners, and the owners of the container ship being towed by the David Lawrence.

After answers were filed, attorneys for Sergant Lockwood filed

39 interrogatories directed to Lawrence Partnership, Ltd. The 38th interrogatory read: "State whether any statements of the members of the crews of the Tugboat David Lawrence or of any other vessel were taken in connection with the towing of the container ship and the sinking of the David Lawrence." The interrogatory was accompanied by a Request to Produce which requested: "Attach hereto exact copies of statements of members of the crew or any other person taken in connection with the towing of the container ship and the sinking of the David Lawrence if in writing, and if oral, set forth in detail the exact provisions of any such oral statements or reports." Further, supplemental interrogatories asked additional questions: Supplemental question 3 asked whether any oral or written statements, records, reports or other memoranda had been made concerning any matter relative to the towing operation, the sinking of the tug, the salvaging and repair of the tug, and the death of the deceased. If the answer was in the affirmative, the tug owners were then requested to set forth the nature of all such records, reports, statements or other memoranda. Supplemental question 4 asked for the names of all persons "interviewed by the owners of the tug boat David Lawrence or by anyone conducting interviews on their behalf."

Lawrence Partnership, Ltd., through attorney Anson, answered all of the interrogatories except No. 38 and supplemental question 3. While admitting that statements of the survivors had been taken, Anson declined to summarize or set forth the contents. Anson did so on the ground that such requests called "for privileged matter obtained in preparation for litigation" and constituted protected work product.

Questions

1. Are statements made by members of the crew of the tugboat David Lawrence to attorney Arnold Anson, who represents the Lawrence Partnership, Ltd. "relevant" for discovery purposes under Rule 26(b)(1)?

2. Are these same statements privileged within the meaning of Rule 26(b)(1)?

3 As to statements made by crew members who became parties to any of the lawsuits either before the Steamboat Inspectors or to attorney Anson, can those parties obtain their own statements? How?

4. Assume that Counsel for Sergant Lockwood has moved to sanction the owners of the David Lawrence and counsel Anson for discovery abuse.

    A. Can the owners of the David Lawrence refuse to answer, on Rule 26(b)(3) work product grounds, the interrogatory question: "State whether any statements of the members of the crews of the Tugboat David Lawrence or of any other vessel were taken in connection with the towing of the container ship and the sinking of the David Lawrence?" If so, on what grounds?

    B. Can the owners of the David Lawrence refuse to produce, on Rule 26(b)(3) work product grounds, written statements of witnesses or crew members?

C. Are there any Rule 26(b)(3) issues with supplemental question 4 asking which persons counsel interviewed?

Disclosure of Expert Witnesses–
Non-Retained Experts

Herr v. Blackwell

Rudolph Herr, a citizen of Georgia, made an appointment with and was first examined by Dr. Stephen Blackwell approximately seven years ago. As part of this routine examination, Dr. Blackwell ordered a Prostate Specific Antigen ("PSA") test. A nurse in Dr. Blackwell's office informed Mr. Herr that the results of the PSA were slightly elevated and that Mr. Herr should have the test repeated in two months. Mr. Herr did not return to Dr. Blackwell to have the PSA test repeated.

Five years ago, as a result of insurance changes, Mr. Herr selected a new primary care physician. This physician performed a routine physical examination and ordered a PSA test. The test indicated that Mr. Herr's PSA was high and accordingly, the physician referred Mr. Herr to a urologist, who conducted a biopsy that revealed prostate cancer. Mr. Herr was then treated through external radiation by a radiation oncologist, Dr. Gwendolyn Teeter. Dr. Teeter treated Mr. Herr for approximately 18 months.

Rudolph Herr and his wife Sandy, filed suit against Dr. Blackwell in the United States District Court for the Northern District of Florida because Dr. Blackwell was a citizen of Florida whose practice was located near Gainesville. The Herrs alleged that Dr. Blackwell provided inadequate care and treatment by (1) failing to inform Mr. Herr that a PSA test was abnormally elevated and (2) failing to recommend that Mr. Herr undergo further testing or follow-up treatment.

During discovery, the parties sought information about non-retained experts. Dr. Blackwell responded to one such question by indicating that he "may call Gwendolyn Teeter, M.D. to testify regarding her care and treatment of Mr. Herr which may include causation testimony and testimony regarding prognosis."

Three days before trial, the Herrs filed a Motion to Strike Witness Dr. Teeter, M.D. In support of their motions, the Herrs alleged (a) Dr. Teeter was no longer a treating physician/non-retained expert because Dr. Teeter reviewed his own records, several depositions in the case and several articles to confirm the correctness of his treatment and (b) Dr. Blackwell failed to disclose that Dr. Teeter was a retained expert within the meaning of Rule 26(a)(2)(B)

Questions

1. What is a "retained" expert within the meaning of Rule 26(a)(2)(B)?
2. If Dr. Teeter is not a "retained" expert, when must she be disclosed as a witness? Is that a fair result?

Retained Experts and Privilege/Work Product

Burrows v. Tar Creek Enterprises, Inc.

Jonathan Burrows, a citizen of Oklahoma, was one of twenty-six persons who allegedly suffered personal injuries caused by exposure to lead resulting from lead and zinc mining operations conducted by Tar Creek Enterprises, Inc., a corporate citizen of Delaware. Burrows and the others filed suit in the correct United States District Court asserting claims for negligence, strict liability and nuisance. In order to evaluate their medical claims in this litigation, all twenty six plaintiffs were examined by neuropsychologists Jon Bonny and Hazel Forrest. It was anticipated that Drs. Bonny and Forrest's examination would lead to each of them offering expert opinions about the Plaintiffs' condition at trial. As a result, when each of the Plaintiffs was examined, each of the Plaintiffs agreed to have their records reviewed by Drs. Bonny and Forrest when the doctors prepared their expert testimony. As a result, the medical records of all of the Plaintiffs were shared with the doctors and were used by them in forming their opinions. After these medical examinations, however, nineteen of the original plaintiffs dismissed their claims and were removed as parties to the lawsuit. As a result, in response to Rule 26(a)(2)(B), counsel for the Plaintiffs submitted to the attorneys for Tar Creek the examination reports of Drs. Bonny and Forrest for the seven remaining Plaintiffs.

Thereafter, attorneys for Tar Creek demanded Drs. Bonny and Forrest's medical records with respect to all 26 original plaintiffs--the remaining Plaintiffs *and* the dismissed Plaintiffs. Plaintiffs refused to provide documents relating to the dismissed Plaintiffs, claiming that the dismissed Plaintiffs medical records; (1) are irrelevant to the claims or defenses of any party since the dismissed Plaintiffs no longer assert any claim herein; (2) are protected by physician-patient privilege; and, (3) are protected work product.

Question

You may assume that the court ruled that the records of Drs. Bonny and Forrest relating to the nineteen dismissed Plaintiffs must be turned over to the defendants. State the reasoning of the District Court as to each of the Plaintiffs' three claims regarding these records.

Discovery Sanctions

Schecter v. FoodFresh, Inc.

Laurie Schecter, a former employee of FoodFresh Inc., filed a Complaint in a correct United States District Court alleging claims of race, gender and age discrimination against FoodFresh pursuant to Title VII of the federal Civil Rights Act and federal Age Discrimination in Employment Act. Following an Answer, Ms. Schecter refused to submit her mandatory disclosures pursuant to Rule 26(a)(1). Over the course of the next eight months, FoodFresh sent her four different letters, all of which went unanswered and were thereafter followed by FoodFresh's motion for sanctions. The court refused those sanctions and ordered Schecter to file her mandatory disclosures.

Thereafter, FoodFresh sent Ms. Schecter a set of interrogatories and requests for production. When she did not respond to FoodFresh's discovery requests by the due date, counsel for FoodFresh sent her a certified letter requesting that she provide both her overdue disclosures and responses to the delinquent discovery requests within twenty days. Rather than provide the information, Ms. Schecter telephoned counsel for FoodFresh on the twenty-first day and stated that she could not meet the deadlines because she had been out of town attending a funeral and the individual who prepared her legal papers was unavailable for ten days. Counsel for FoodFresh agreed to allow Ms. Schecter an additional fifteen days to provide this information. However, as of thirty days later, no responses or disclosures were forthcoming. FoodFresh then filed a motion for sanctions requesting that the district court dismiss Ms. Schecter's case. That motion was not presented to the court for decision.

In an effort to obtain information about the case, counsel for FoodFresh sent Ms. Schecter a letter asking her for available dates the following month when she would be available for deposition. Ms. Schecter did not respond. As a result, FoodFresh noticed her deposition for a date several weeks later. Ms. Schecter did not appear for her deposition causing FoodFresh to incur a court reporter fee.

FoodFresh sent Ms. Schecter a second notice to appear for a deposition scheduled to occur approximately six months later. About two weeks in advance of the new date, Ms. Schecter filed two motions, one requesting that her deposition be postponed because she would "be represented in the future by new counsel," and the other requesting a 90-day extension of the discovery cut-off "so that she could have an attorney represent her in court."

The United States Magistrate presiding over the case denied Ms.

Schecter's request to postpone her deposition and granted her request to extend the discovery deadline. The Magistrate Judge instructed Ms. Schecter to cooperate with FoodFresh in its efforts to obtain discovery and warned her that if she failed or refused to cooperate, the court could order that sanctions be imposed upon her in the form of attorneys' fees or the dismissal of her claims.

Ms. Schecter did appear for her depositions but, by the time she did, she still had not provided her disclosures or discovery responses. Accordingly, FoodFresh filed another motion for sanctions, requesting that the court dismiss the action with prejudice and award FoodFresh its attorneys' fees and costs caused by Ms. Schecter's repeated failure to cooperate with discovery.

Five days after FoodFresh filed its motion for sanctions and 10 days before the extended discovery cut-off, Ms. Schecter sent FoodFresh her responses to FoodFresh's interrogatories and document requests. In her responses, for example, FoodFresh asked Ms. Schecter to identify the "younger white co-worker with less time in service" that Ms. Schecter used for comparative purposes for her age discrimination claims. In her answer, Ms. Schecter responded that "defendant can get the identity of the younger, white co-worker itself from the company promotion revised list." Additionally, FoodFresh asked the same question with regard to another promotion which she alleged in her Complaint that she was discriminatorily denied, to which Ms. Schecter responded, "the defendant can use the same promotion list stated in the prior answer." The promotion list in question identifies seven employees promoted in the relevant period, all of whom are younger than Plaintiff and six of whom are white. Further, Ms. Schecter's responses to FoodFresh's interrogatories identified two witnesses whom she had not previously disclosed, a labor economist and a treating physician. The expert designation deadline had expired six months prior to the date that she served her discovery responses.

With regard to FoodFresh's document requests, Ms. Schecter claimed in her response to FoodFresh's motion for sanctions that she no longer had the documents "due to the fact that [she] had put all her belongings in storage and could not make payments on the storage" and, thus, the documents were "auctioned off."

FoodFresh again renewed its motion for dismissal and/or sanctions. The court found that dismissal of Ms. Schecter's claims was not appropriate because monetary and evidentiary sanctions would "remedy, in large part, the prejudice suffered by [FoodFresh]." Accordingly, the court directed Ms. Schecter to pay FoodFresh's attorneys' fees in connection with its motion for sanctions and prohibited Ms. Schecter from introducing at trial any fact or assertion that she had not previously provided to FoodFresh during the discovery process. In addition, the district court indicated that it would give a spoliation of evidence instruction at trial with respect to the documents in storage which Ms. Schecter claimed were "auctioned off." The district court warned Ms. Schecter that if she failed to make payment when directed by the court, it would dismiss the action.

Pursuant to the district court's Order, FoodFresh submitted its statement of attorneys' fees and the court ordered Ms. Schecter to pay sanctions in the amount of $2,107 within 20 days of the Order. The court informed Ms. Schecter that "failure to strictly comply with [the] Order will result in dismissal of her case." One day after this payment was due, Ms. Schecter filed a motion entitled "Motion For Jury Trial of Right under Seventh Amendment of United States Constitution." Ms. Schecter's motion made no mention of the district court's order directing her to pay sanctions or her failure to comply with that Order. Three months later, FoodFresh filed a motion to dismiss Ms. Schecter's case with prejudice on the grounds that the deadline for her to comply with the court's Order by paying FoodFresh's attorneys' fees had passed and that, pursuant to the court's admonition to Schecter, her case should be dismissed.

Questions

1. When were Ms. Schecter's mandatory disclosures due under Rule 26(a)(1)?

2. Discuss the district court's original sanction order, in which Ms. Schecter was required to pay attorney's fees, barred from introducing evidence not disclosed and told that the court would give a "spoilation" instruction.

3. Discuss what the court might do on the current motion.

4. Discuss what the court might have done to prevent discovery in this case from reaching the level it reached.

CHAPTER 8

RESOLUTION PRIOR TO TRIAL

Settlement/Consent Decrees

United States v. Brotherhood of Electrical Contractors

Sometime ago, the Attorney General, on behalf of the United States, sued the Brotherhood of Electrical Contractors or BEC. and the BEC's General Executive Board. The BEC is an international union whose members work primarily in the building construction trade. The purpose of the United States lawsuit was, according to the Attorney General, to rid the BEC of the "hideous influence of organized crime." The suit was filed under civil provisions of federal racketeering laws and was filed in an appropriate federal district court.

After considerable negotiations, the United States and the BEC agreed to resolve the dispute and did so by way of a Consent Decree that was approved by the federal trial court. Among other reforms, the Consent Decree restructured the BEC's electoral system to provide for direct, secret-ballot, rank-and-file election of the union's top officers, so that the union's elections could be free of "unlawful outside influence." The Consent Decree appointed an independent Election Officer, Elaine Weinstein, and provided for payment of her by the United States. The Decree then permanently enjoined all of the union's officers, representatives, members and employees from committing any acts of racketeering activity and obstructing or otherwise interfering with the work of the Court-appointed officers or a separately appointed Independent Review Board. Following the Consent Decree, and pursuant to it, the BEC's first-ever direct, rank-and-file election was held under the supervision of Election Officer Weinstein.

The election concluded with an announcement of the winning candidates for various offices. Following the announcements, post-election protests were filed. Election Officer Weinstein conducted an investigation of the post-election protests and uncovered serious violations of the Election Rules including numerous attempts to improperly influence the election both by the union and by certain employers. As a result, the Election Officer granted certain post-election protests, finding that the violations of the Election Rules "may have affected the outcome of the election." She refused to certify the election results, ordered a rerun election for all positions, and disqualified some candidates from running for office because of their participation in the election's corruption.

To fund the rerun election, Election Officer Weinstein filed a motion in the district court seeking some $7.4 million in funds. The original election, at a cost of approximately $18 million was funded entirely by the United States through various appropriations measures.

At the hearing on her motion, Election Officer Weinstein did not argue that BEC should be required to fund the rerun election, but did argue that the new election was not the fault of the United States.

Election Officer Weinstein pointed out to the court that there was but limited federal sources to pay for the new election. While the Consent Decree called for initial government funding of BEC elections, legislation authorizing funding for BEC election in prior fiscal years specifically prevented ongoing funding of future BEC election activities.

In response, the BEC argued that despite what Congress had done, the Government must still pay for the rerun election. The BEC claimed that it "entered into the Consent Decree with 'the United States,' not with a branch of government; the underlying suit was brought and settled in the name of 'the United States,' and the Court's decree runs to and binds 'the United States.' " Therefore, the BEC contended that it was the entire government's obligation, and not the obligation of the Court, the Election Officer, or the BEC, to find funding for the rerun election. The BEC countered the Government's suggestion that the BEC pay the cost of the rerun election by arguing that the Consent Decree did not require supervision over the initial election, providing only that if the United States opted to supervise the election, it must do so at its own expense. Further, the BEC contended that no legal authority permitted a later transfer of financial obligations from the United States to the BEC because "[t]he Consent Decree cannot be interpreted to accommodate such a radical revision of the bargain made by the parties, particularly because the financial obligation of the United States arises only because the United States elected to supervise the election."

In its ruling, the District Court made the following points:

★ Prior to the entry of the Consent Decree, the BEC was plagued with corruption and the influences of organized crime, devoid of any democratic traditions. The goal of the Consent Decree was to rid the BEC of these hideous influences.

★ Indeed, in the decades prior to the entry of the Consent

Decree, the Government, at a cost of tens of millions of dollars, obtained convictions against approximately 340 individuals in more than 200 prosecutions involving BEC-related corruption.

★ The Consent Decree's electoral reforms made possible the first democratic, rank-and-file elections in the union's history and produced extraordinary participation by union members.

★ The Government has long understood that only a continued effort would accomplish the long-standing objective of ridding the BEC of corruption and the infiltration of organized crime.

★ The rerun election is a conti nuation of the original election. Paragraph 12(D)(ix) of the Consent Decree clearly states that "[t]he union defendants consent to the Election Officer, at Government expense, to supervise the BEC elections."

★ The parties agree that in order to achieve these goals, a supervised rerun election is imperative.

To fund the rerun election, the United States argued that the court had "inherent authority to enter reasonable orders to ensure compliance with a consent decree." Such authority enabled the Court to order the BEC to bear the cost of the rerun election, particularly in light of the finding of the neutral Election Officer that union officers, acting in their official capacity had caused the need for the rerun election. The activities of these officers, according to the Government, should be attributed to the union itself.

In its ruling, the court found that a consent decree is an order of the court and thus, by its very nature, vests the court with equitable discretion to enforce the obligations imposed on the parties. The court further found that although supervision of the rerun election was clearly in the public interest, the Consent Decree did not impose a legal duty on the Government to continue indefinitely to have the election process supervised at the Government's expense. According to the court, the Government had already expended over $17.5 million on the original BEC Election in order to achieve the goals of the Consent Decree. Because additional costs were now needed due to the actions taken by persons affiliated with and acting for the BEC, the court found it equitable to require that the BEC bear the additional costs caused by its own conduct. The court indicated that BEC made the mess and had the job to clean it up.

Questions

1. Given the lengthy history of abuse by the BEC, and particularly the convictions already obtained by the United States, why would the government, or any party for that matter, be willing to enter

into a Consent Decree?

    2. What is the legal nature of a Consent Decree? Assume that one party violates the Consent Decree and the other party brings an independent action in court to remedy that violation. What will be the legal nature of that action?

    3. Do you agree with the court that the Consent Decree is an Order of the court and thus vests the court with the power to enforce it? If not, what should be the role of the trial judge in enforcing consent decrees or other settlements?

    4. Assume you are the law clerk for the Court of Appeals judge to whom this case is assigned. Do you think the trial judge here went too far? Why or why not?

Voluntary Dismissal

As of Right

Universal Soccer, Inc. v. Kingston Industries, Inc.

    Universal Soccer Company, Inc., a California corporation, has sold soccer equipment, uniforms, and other soccer-related merchandise for over ten years under the trademark "Back of the Net" and bearing a "Back of the Net" logo. Recently, Kingston Industries, Inc., an Oregon corporation, formed a division named "Back of the Net Now," which began selling sports clothing with logos containing the words "Back of the Net Now." After it learned that Back of the Net Now was selling clothing bearing the "Back of the Net Now" logo, Universal Soccer filed a complaint alleging trademark infringement and unfair competition, requesting a jury trial, and seeking a temporary restraining order. The district court denied the application for a temporary restraining order the same day without a hearing. Universal Soccer then filed a motion for a preliminary injunction. Back of the Net Now requested, and Universal Soccer stipulated to, an extension of time for Back of the Net Now to respond. The court approved the extension, and, pursuant to its authority under Fed.R.Civ.P. 65(a)(2), sua sponte consolidated the preliminary injunction hearing with the trial. The parties thereafter conducted expedited discovery, including depositions and document production, and Back of the Net Now filed motions in limine to exclude evidence. When the parties appeared for the preliminary injunction hearing/trial, the district court announced "this matter is going to proceed as a motion for summary judgment, cross-motions for summary judgment." Universal Soccer asserted its right to a jury trial, but the district court continued without addressing the issue. Over two days and seven hours, both sides introduced exhibits and examined witnesses. At the end of testimony, the district court did not allow summation, instead directing the parties to present "material facts that they believe are without contest to prove their case or to grant the summary judgment to that party." The court also asked for post-trial briefs stating that when the briefs were filed "I'll make a determination as to whether or not I need any further hearing in the matter."

The day after the hearing ended, Universal Soccer filed a notice of voluntary dismissal.

Question

What happens now? Why?

By Motion

Howard v. InterContinental Airlines

Douglas Howard was a private in the United States Army. He was reported missing from his unit in the Netherlands and eventually declared to be Absent Without Leave (AWOL). After 30 days on AWOL status, Howard was dropped from the rolls of his unit. When he later attempted to return to his unit. He was arrested and transported from Europe to the United States by commercial flights first on World Airlines, a Delaware corporation and then on InterContinental Airlines, a Minnesota corporation. There is no issue but that Howard did not suffer any physical injuries on any of these flights or during his time in confinement.

Sometime thereafter, Douglas Howard filed a civil suit in the correct federal district court against World Airlines, InterContinental Airlines, and numerous U.S. Army Defendants for kidnaping. Upon filing its answer, defendant InterContinental Airlines moved for summary judgment, on the grounds that Howard's complaint was filed outside the time permitted by the applicable statute of limitations. InterContinental's answer and summary judgment papers contained numerous factual statements concerning Howard's disappearance, and subsequent return, to his Army unit. In addition, the U.S. Army Defendants moved to dismiss plaintiff's complaint primarily because of the doctrine established in *Feres v. United States,* 340 U.S. 135, 71 S.Ct. 153, 95 L.Ed. 152 (1950), a doctrine which bars military personnel from suing the United States or other service members for alleged torts that occur "in the course of activity incident to service."

Following the filing of these motions, Douglas Howard filed another action in the proper federal district court. This action was against InterContinental Airlines and both the attorney and the law firm that represented InterContinental Airlines in the kidnaping case. In this second action, Howard alleged that InterContinental and its lawyers defamed him by insinuating in InterContinental Airlines' motion papers in the kidnaping action that charges of desertion were being considered against him. After answering, InterContinental moved to dismiss the defamation action for failure to state a claim alleging the claim to be barred by absolute privilege because it arose in connection with a judicial proceeding. The defendants also moved for sanctions against the plaintiff pursuant to Fed.R.Civ.P. 11.

Before the Court could rule on InteContinental's motion to dismiss in the defamation action, Howard moved to dismiss without prejudice both the kidnaping and the defamation actions as against all defendants. This motion was opposed by both the U.S. Army Defendants and defendant InterContinental Airlines, who contend that said dismissal should be entered with prejudice, thereby precluding the institution of a new lawsuit concerning the same claims. In the alternative, defendant InterContinental Airlines requests attorney's fees and costs should the Court approve plaintiff's application for voluntary dismissal without prejudice.

Questions

1. Why is a motion for voluntary dismissal necessary?
2. You may assume that the *Feres* doctrine will almost certainly bar the kidnaping action against the U.S. Army and that privilege will bar the defamation action. Why should the court even consider the motion to dismiss? Why not simply grant the summary judgment by the Army and the dismissal motion by InterContinental?
3. What factors should the court consider in ruling on the motion seeking dismissal without prejudice?
4. How should the court handle the request for attorneys' fees?

Involuntary Dismissal

Landon v. Northwestern State University

Matthew Landon, a citizen of Illinois, was a student at Northwestern State University, a corporate citizen of Vermont. While a student, Landon was involved in an automobile accident in which he suffered serious head injuries. Upon returning to the University, Landon requested accommodation for his injury-related learning difficulties under the Americans with Disability Act.

Approximately two years after his return to school, Landon filed suit in the correct federal district court against Northwestern State University alleging violations of the Americans with Disabilities Act and the Rehabilitation Act, both federal laws. Landon claimed that the University neglected his needs and failed to provide the accommodations that he requested or, alternatively, provided inadequate accommodations. Following the filing of the complaint, the case proceeded over a several year period. Thereafter, the district court dismissed Landon's claim with prejudice, pursuant to Rule 41(b).

In dismissing the complaint, the district court found as follows:

First, Landon failed to comply in a timely fashion with the district court's order to produce certain material documents (specifically, bank and income tax records) that appellees had sought unsuccessfully from appellant since the beginning of the action. Instead, appellant sporadically produced selected documents, some of which were not produced until the day of the hearing on the district court's order to show cause why the action should not be dismissed for appellant's violation of discovery orders.

Second, appellant failed to appear at a properly-noticed, court-ordered deposition.

Finally, appellant violated a court order prohibiting him from firing his fourth set of counsel. Specifically, during a scheduling conference, the district court forewarned appellant via his then-current counsel, Lynn Bastion, that his case would be dismissed with prejudice if he should fire her. The following exchange occurred:

> THE COURT: If this guy fires you Lynn [Bastion], I'm going to dismiss his case with prejudice.
>
> MS. Bastion: Okay. I understand that, Your Honor.
>
> THE COURT: You better tell him that.
>
> MS. Bastion: Okay. I understand that, Your Honor.

Bastion subsequently informed appellant in writing that her withdrawal would trigger the dismissal of his case with prejudice. Specifically, Bastion wrote: "The Judge said that if your lawyers withdraw again, he will dismiss the case with prejudice. I just want you to be aware of that." Despite this warning, soon after receipt of the letter, Landon fired Bastion. By that time, four sets of counsel had withdrawn and been replaced as attorneys-of-record in the case. As a result of these changes in counsel and the new issues raised in several amended complaints filed by Landon and the new lawyers, the district court extended the discovery cut-off date five times and reset the trial date three times.

The motion to dismiss granted by the court was the second filed by the University. The court had previously denied a motion filed by the University under Rule 41(b) after Landon had not filed timely responses to discovery.

Landon has appealed the dismissal with prejudice.

Questions

1. When Rule 41(b) speaks of a dismissal "upon the merits," what does that mean?

2. What factors should the court consider in ruling on a motion to dismiss under Rule 41(b)?

3. Did the district court correctly rule in this case?

Default

Heritage Bank v. LaRoush

Adam LaRoush, a citizen of Nevada and now a resident of Japan, was a representative of Secon Industries, Inc., a Hong Kong corporation in the business of obtaining engineering contracts and then subcontracting the entire project. In that regard, Secon Industries contracted with Quito-San Lorenzo, an Ecuador corporation to renovate a railroad line in that country. The contract required Secon to prepare or procure drawings, surveys, and specifications for the project and to furnish a list of needed equipment and materials. Secon, by subcontract, engaged the Harmatsu Construction Company, a Japanese corporation, to perform on behalf of Secon the engineering studies for Quito-San Lorenzo. The subcontract obligated Secon to make periodic payments to Harmatsu for, among other things, salaries and expenditures paid in connection with the project. To finance these payments, Secon, through Adam LaRoush, negotiated with the Heritage National Bank, a Texas corporation, to obtain a letter of credit in favor of Harmatsu for the account of Secon. The bank recognized that Secon would be able to cover drafts by Harmatsu against the letter of credit only if Quito-San Lorenzo, satisfied with the work, paid Secon. The terms of the letter of credit therefore required that all drafts bear the countersignature of Adam LaRoush or another authorized representative of Secon, to show Secon's approval of the payment and to certify that the listed expenses had preliminary approval. Moreover, the bank sought to protect itself by taking an assignment of Secon's rights under the contract with Quito-San Lorenzo as security for its issuance of credit on behalf of Secon.

Everything went smoothly for six months, and the first seven drafts submitted by Harmatsu were honored by the bank. They had been countersigned on behalf of Secon as follows: "/s/ Adam LaRoush, on behalf of Secon, Ind., Inc." The bank refused, however, to honor the next nine drafts because, it said, it had received inadequate documentation of the expenses and because it had learned that in spite of Secon's and Harmatsu's certification to the contrary, Quito-San Lorenzo had refused to give preliminary approval to the invoices. Harmatsu sued Heritage National Bank in the federal court in Texas to recover under the letter of credit. The bank answered, denying its liability. The bank also filed a third-party complaint against Secon and Adam LaRoush. The third party complaint alleged first that Adam LaRoush and Secon, under the agreement executed in connection with the application for a letter of credit were obligated to reimburse the bank for any sums paid Harmatsu under that letter of credit. The bank also joined a claim against Secon and Adam LaRoush on a demand promissory note.

Secon and Adam LaRoush filed no responsive pleadings. Heritage Bank and Harmatsu, however, settled the controversy between them and, on motion of these two parties, the court dismissed the main claim. The bank then requested the clerk of the district court to enter the default of Secon and Adam LaRoush for their failure to plead or otherwise defend the third-party action. A copy of this request was forwarded to Adam LaRoush. The bank later filed a motion for a default judgment, and a copy of the motion was forwarded to Adam LaRoush and Secon in Tokyo. The court granted the motion.

Questions

1. Assume that Heritage Bank requested the clerk of the court to enter the default of Adam LaRoush and that request was forwarded to Adam LaRoush. What could LaRoush do, at that stage, to try and get into the case? What standards/rules would govern any attempt he made?

2. What is the difference between the clerk entering default and the request for a default judgment?

3. When the clerk has entered a default, but there is not yet a default judgment, what does that mean? Can LaRoush still contest any part of the proceeding? If so, what?

4. The problem says that Heritage Bank moved for the entry of default? Why would that be necessary under Rule 55 in this case? What could the bank have done in the alternative? Why?

5. Assume that the court went ahead and entered a default judgment against LaRoush for $82,208 plus costs and attorneys' fees. If LaRoush wants the trial court to reconsider that judgment, what rule will LaRoush use to proceed?

6. Assume that the court entered a default judgment and that LaRoush's first activity in the action was to file an appeal of the trial court's decision. What can LaRoush challenge? Will he be successful in this case? Why or why not?

Summary Judgment

Waddle v. Central Railroad Co.

James and Marie Waddle are husband and wife and citizens of Kentucky. The Central Railroad Co. is a railroad company with passenger and freight lines around the country. It is a corporate citizen of Kentucky. In September, three years ago, James and Marie Waddle were passengers on a Central Railroad train heading from Pittsburgh to

Louisville. As a result of the negligence of the railroad, Marie Waddle was injured in an accident while on the train. Lawyers for the railroad immediately contacted the Waddles and worked out a settlement. In exchange for the Waddles agreeing not to sue the railroad, the railroad granted to the Waddles unlimited passenger access on the Central Railroad and any railroad affiliated with the Central Railroad for the remainder of the life of the older survivor of James and Marie Waddle. After agreeing to this settlement, the Waddles signed a release in favor of the railroad.

Almost one year after this settlement, Congress became aware of several abuses practiced by railroad companies, including the use of free railroad passenger passes to members of Congress and other elected officials. Apparently Congress believed that these free passes were provided to legislative members as a means of unduly influencing these legislators in the lawful performance of their duties. As a result, Congress adopted legislation prohibiting any railroad within the United States from honoring any free access passes.

When the Waddles were advised that the railroad would no longer honor their unlimited access because of the Congressional enactment, the Waddles sued the railroad. The suit was filed in the United States District Court in Kentucky and alleged that the railroad was in breach of its contract with the Waddles for the provision of free access to the railroad. The suit also alleged the act of Congress did not prohibit the giving of passes under the circumstances of this case; and, second, that, if the Congressional enactment did so prohibit, then the law was in conflict with the 5th Amendment of the Constitution, because it deprived the plaintiffs of their property without due process of law.

Questions

This problem may remind you of *Louisville & Nashville R.R. v. Mottley*, 211 U.S. 149 (1908), which you may have read in studying Subject Matter Jurisdiction. Assume first that the railroad first moved to dismiss, for want of subject matter jurisdiction. Now assume that, for whatever reason, that motion was denied. Assume now that the defendant moves for summary judgment. Articulate how this new motion is different from a motion to dismiss.

1. How is summary judgment like a trial? How is it different?

2. If a party is successful in seeking Summary Judgment, how is that party better off than the party who is able to be successful on the motion to dismiss?

3. As to the party losing summary judgment, how will that party gain review of the summary judgment grant?

Claret v. Reliable Construction, Inc.

Noel and Ronald Claret were husband and wife and citizens of Alabama. Stirrat Corporation is a corporate citizen of Georgia and instals insulation in commercial and residential structures. Ronald Claret served as Executive Vice President of the Downtown Cultural Club in Opelika, Alabama. When the Downtown Cultural Club wanted to build a new office building for itself, it hired Reliable Construction, Inc., another Georgia corporation to be the general contractor. After the building was built, the Downtown Cultural Club and Ronald Claret maintained their offices in the new building. Within several years, however, Ronald Claret was diagnosed with Mesothelioma, a deadly disease almost always caused by inhalation of asbestos from decaying insulation. When Ronald Claret died within about a year after his diagnosis, Noel Claret hired investigators and had the insulation from the Downtown Cultural Club tested for asbestos. When this testing proved positive and her medical experts were satisfied that Ronald Claret's Mesothelioma was likely caused by his close exposure to the asbestos in the insulation, Noel Claret filed suit in the United States District court in Georgia against Reliable Construction, Inc., the general contractor on the Cultural Club project. Reliable's records were no longer available because of a fire in their offices shortly after the completion of the Cultural Center, so it was unclear who had manufactured and installed the insulation for the project. As a result, Noel Claret sued Stirrat Corporation and several other companies that her investigation revealed had regularly provided insulation to Reliable during the period immediately preceding construction of the Downtown Cultural Club. These lawsuits all sounded in negligence, strict liability and breach of warranty.

Questions

1.   Assume that Noel Claret's claim against Reliable Construction, Inc. is a claim that sounds very similar to a res ipsa loquitur claim. Claret argues that as general contractor, Reliable was responsible for the entire construction project; that asbestos was installed under Reliable's supervision and that Ronald Claret died of exposure to asbestos. As a result, Noel Claret's lawyers want to file for summary judgment against Reliable Construction, Inc.

   A.   What is the earliest time that Claret can file this motion?

   B.   What specifically must Claret prove to be able to obtain summary judgment against Reliable?

2. Assume that Stirrat Corporation sent interrogatories to Noel Claret. One of those interrogatories asked: "Please list the names of any persons who might have information showing that Ronald Claret was exposed to insulation provided or installed by Stirrat Corporations." In

her response, Noel Claret indicated: "None known at this time." As a result, Stirrat Corporation's lawyer now wants to move for summary judgment.

    A. What is the earliest time that Stirrat Corporation can file this motion?

    B.   What documents do you anticipate Stirrat Corporation's lawyers will file?

    C. Stirrat's lawyers argue that they are entitled to summary judgment because Claret cannot show that Ronald Claret was exposed to asbestos installed or provided by Stirrat Corporation. Is this enough or must Stirrat show that it did not provide such asbestos?

    3. How can the court consider summary judgment for Stirrat when there are other defendants in the case? What will happen to the action against any of them?

    4.   Assume that Stirrat's lawyers present Noel Claret's interrogatory answer indicating that she did not know of anyone who had knowledge of her husband being exposed to insulation supplied or installed by Stirrat.

    A. Can Claret successfully argue that at trial she will attempt to present evidence that Stirrat supplied or installed asbestos to the Cultural Center project? Why or why not?

    B. Can Claret successfully argue that her husband's deposition, taken shortly before his death, reveals his belief that it was Stirrat that supplied or installed the insulation? Why or why not?

    C. Can Claret successfully present an affidavit from her lawyer that the lawyer has talked to several witnesses who will be available to testify at trial who will say that they saw Stirrat Corporation trucks at the worksite at the time of the Cultural Center's construction? Why or why not?

    D. Can Claret successfully present an affidavit from a person who was President of Reliable Construction who will say that to the best of his knowledge, information and belief, it was Stirrat Corporation who supplied or installed the insulation on the Cultural Center construction? Why or why not?

    5. Assume that Claret does present an affidavit of the person who was President of Reliable Construction and the affidavit indicates that to the best of his knowledge, information and belief, it was Stirrat Corporation who supplied or installed the insulation on the Cultural Center construction. Stirrat Corporation then presents affidavits from every person who was a foreperson of the Corporation at the time of the Cultural Center construction and that each of those eight affidavits says that Stirrat did not supply or install insulation on the Cultural Center site. Is summary judgment now appropriate for Stirrat? Why or why not?

CHAPTER 9

THE PROCEDURE OF TRIALS

Continuances

Defenders of Nature, Inc. v. Central School District

Defenders of Nature, Inc. is a Colorado based charitable organization whose members fund and conduct environmental litigation. The Central School District of Tucson, Arizona, is the duly elected school district operating the public schools within the city. In furtherance of their charge, the School District paid $1.78 million to purchase a 73 acre site in northwest Tucson, Arizona upon which a new high school would be built. The high school complex is intended to accommodate 2,100 students and is composed of several buildings, athletic fields and parking areas for students, faculty and visitors. Following the School District's purchase of the school site, the United States Fish and Wildlife Service, following proper federal procedure, formally listed the pygmy-owl as an endangered species under federal law. The pygmy-owl is a small reddish brown owl known for its relatively long tail and monotonous call which is heard primarily at dawn and dusk. The pygmy-owl nests in a cavity of a large tree or large columnar cactus. Its habitats include areas from lowland central Arizona south through portions of western Mexico and from southern Texas south through other portions of Mexico on down through portions of Central America. The Fish and Wildlife Service found that there were some 54,400 acres of suitable pygmy-owl habitat in northwest Tucson. This included the 73 acre school site. In fact, the school site falls within an area designated as critical habitat for the pygmy-owl.

When the School District began salvaging operations as a precursor to beginning construction, Defenders of Nature, which had been following the School Board's activities, filed suit in the proper federal district court in Tucson seeking a temporary restraining order and a preliminary injunction against the School District to prevent any action on the school site, claiming that any construction would likely harm or harass a pygmy-owl. The district court entered a temporary restraining order and consolidated the hearing on Defenders' request for a preliminary injunction with the trial on the merits.

While awaiting a hearing on the merits, the parties engaged in discovery, including discovery of the opinions of experts.

As a result, when the hearing on the merits took place, Defenders was not surprised that the School Board called Mary Daniels, a consultant to testify. Defenders, was, however, apparently surprised by Ms. Daniels' testimony. Daniels indicated that based upon her survey of the site, conducted three days before trial, there were no pygmy-owls occupying the proposed high school property owned by the School District. Daniels also testified that she did, in fact, see one small owl with eggs in a saguaro cavity on the property, but that she concluded it was an elf owl rather than a pygmy-owl. Daniels further indicated that she returned to the site the following day to verify that she had in fact seen an elf owl rather than a pygmy-owl because distinguishing between the two is often difficult. She verified that she did see an elf owl.

Following this testimony, Defenders sought a continuance to allow them a few extra days to conduct an independent investigation of the saguaro cavities on the site since Daniels had conducted her survey just prior to trial.

Questions

1. Regardless of how the court rules on the request for a continuance, when will the correctness of that decision be reviewed?

2. What does your answer to Question 1 tell you about the standard that a court of appeals will have to use in reviewing the decision by the trial court? What is that standard?

3. Assume you are the trial court. What questions do you have for the attorney for Defenders of Nature? For the attorneys for Central School District?

Right to Jury Trial, the Historical Approach

United States v. AVX, Inc., et als.

The United States and the Commonwealth of Massachusetts filed complaints against AVX, Inc., Belleville Industries, Inc., Aerovox, Inc., RTE Corporation, Cornell-Dubilier Electronics Co., and Federal Pacific Electric Company alleging that each one was liable for polychlorinated biphenyl (PCB) contamination of New Bedford Harbor and the Acushnet River. The lawsuits seek affirmative injunctive relief, clean-up costs, response costs, a declaration of liability for future response costs, recovery for damages to natural resources pursuant to several federal and state statutes and common law theories of liability.

Question

Assuming a jury trial is demanded by all parties, which of the claims, if any, must be tried to a jury?

Johnson v. Georgia Highway Express, Inc.

Richard Johnson was employed by Georgia Highway Express, Inc., an interstate carrier of freight, in the capacity of a 'stripper' and 'stacker' in the appellee's Atlanta terminal. When the company held a meeting with numerous Black employees for the purpose of affording them an opportunity to present grievances to the company, Johnson served as spokesman for the group, inquired of the company how long it would be before Black employees would be allowed to apply for jobs not then held by members of their race. Several weeks after the meeting appellant was discharged from his job. Johnson asserted that his discharge was racially motivated. After completion of an appropriate administrative process, Johnson filed suit under federal law seeking equal employment opportunities without discrimination on the grounds of race or color. The suit sought to enjoin those practices and sought back pay.

Question

Assuming a jury trial is demanded by all parties, which of the claims, if any, must be tried to a jury?

Right to Jury Trial, Analogous Approach

Earl v. Valley Contractors, Inc.

Kathleen Earl was employed by Valley Contractors, Inc. a corporation that regularly participated in federal government contracts. Earl alleged that she was fired from her employment and filed suit against Valley Contractors in federal court alleging discrimination on the basis of age, sex, and retaliation for filing a charge of discrimination. She sued under a little-used federal statute on Human Rights which required her first to take her case to a federal human rights commission. She did so and received a "right to sue" letter from that group. Her complaint sought actual damages including lost wages and emotional distress. Her complaint sought a jury trial.

Question

What type of analysis should the court use in determining Earl's right to jury trial? What result?

Right to Jury Trial, Mixed Claims

Clinical Research, Inc. v. Leonard

Nicholas Leonard, M.D. is a medical doctor and citizen of Pennsylvania who practices in Philadelphia, Pennsylvania. Clinical Research, Inc., a New Jersey corporation, is a research company that arranges for human clinical testing of new drugs.. Pharmaceutical companies contracted with Clinical Research, Inc., to oversee human clinical trials testing new drugs. Clinical, in turn, contracted with Leonard to run several clinical trials for Clinical. The agreements included restrictive covenants that prohibited Leonard from conducting further trials for the pharmaceutical companies for one year following the termination of the consulting agreements unless Clinical served as the intermediary.

The agreement did not work almost from the start. After notifying Clinical approximately two weeks in advance, Leonard terminated the relationship. Thereafter, Clinical filed a six-count petition against Leonard alleging breach of contract, anticipatory repudiation, tortious interference with contracts, and civil conspiracy. Clinical sought preliminary and permanent injunctive relief and damages on every count. In its requests for injunctive relief, Clinical sought to enforce restrictive covenants in the consulting agreements. In response, Leonard filed a four-count counterclaim. He included actions for breach of contract and breach of the implied covenant of good faith and fair dealing. Leonard demanded a jury trial on all claims.

Following a hearing, the trial court denied Clinical's request for a preliminary injunction. The court then indicated that what remained in the case was Clinical's request for a permanent injunction as well as requests for equitable relief and damages and Leonard's claims for breach of contract and breach of the implied covenant of good faith and fair dealing.

Questions

1. Assume Clinical Research, Inc. filed its complaint in the proper federal district court. Will a jury be necessary in the federal court? What will the jury try? When? How will the remaining claims be resolved?

2. Assume Clinical Research, Inc. filed its claim in state court. Although Leonard had properly demanded a jury, the trial court concluded that Leonardi was not entitled to a jury trial because it retained jurisdiction over Radiant's claims pursuant to the equitable cleanup doctrine in that "a court of equity may retain jurisdiction to award damages where equity requires this form of relief in the circumstances."

A.   Is the doctrine contained in *Beacon Theatres* applicable in state court? Why or why not?

B. If the trial judge sat in your state's court, was the trial court correct in its "equitable cleanup" ruling? Why or why not?

Judicial Recusal

Stansfield v. Stansfield

Harold Stansfield had been married to Helen Stansfield for some time. After a very bitter divorce battle, Harold Stansfield was ordered to pay support for both his former wife and his two children. After several years of non-payment, Helen Stansfield filed an action seeking to hold Harold in contempt for failing to make payment. The court heard this petition and, despite Harold's claim that he was unable to financially make any payment, determined that Harold had the present financial ability to pay his wife and children. The court ordered that he do so. Harold refused to pay and another proceeding was filed again seeking to have Harold held in contempt. The trial court had the following interaction with Harold's attorney:

THE COURT: So he's going to tell me one more time he has no money when I haven't believed him anytime before that?

Harold Stansfield's COUNSEL: Well, he's entitled. It's not a matter of what you believe, it's a matter of ...

THE COURT: Unfortunately, I already made those findings, and I don't need his testimony.

Harold Stansfield's COUNSEL: It's a matter of the evidence, Your Honor.

THE COURT: Motion for contempt is granted....

Harold Stansfield then filed a motion to recuse the trial judge. For this problem, you should assume that the state court uses standards identical to 28 U.S.C. §§ 144 and 455.

Questions

1. When must any motion to recuse the trial court be filed?
2. Who will rule on the motion?
3. What is/are the best basis for the motion in this case?
4. Will the motion be granted? Why or why not?

Yarborough v. Valley Coal Company

Billy D. Yarborough was a coal miner for at least thirty years. Yarborough began his employment as a mechanic and welder in one of Valley Coal Company's preparation plants. Yarborough filed a claim for black lung benefits with the Department of Labor under the Federal Coal Mine Health & Safety Act ("Act"), along with a doctor's report indicating that Yarborough was "permanently and totally disabled secondary to the entity of Coal Worker's Pneumoconiosis." Yarborough was then examined by a physician for Valley Coal. His claim was followed by a second claim some time later. As the parties moved through the pre-hearing process, they became engaged in rather heated exchanges about the respective examining physicians. Counsel for Yarborough sought discovery of medical records of Valley's physician in an effort to show bias by that physician in favor of coal companies. Counsel hoped to show that the examining doctor had a long history of referrals from Valley Coal and that the doctor "normally" found factual issues in Valley's favor. In ordering this discovery, the Administrative Law Judge assigned the case wrote: "Based on many years of involvement in expert testimony as an examiner, cross examiner, and administrative law judge, I am convinced that doctors are no less biased by money and by longstanding relations with patients, law firms and the law firms' clients than is anyone else." After noting that Valley Coal's examining doctor testified frequently on behalf of coal mine companies for black lung cases--and specifically, in cases involving Valley's counsel--the ALJ determined that the probative value of the discovery relating to possible bias outweighed the burden of compliance. Valley Coal then sought recusal of the

Administrative Law Judge. You may assume that the administrative review used in the case is entirely proper and that ALJ's are subject to the provisions of 28 U.S.C. §§144 and 455.

Questions

1. What are the best grounds for a recusal motion?
2. Should the Administrative Law Judge be disqualified? Why or why not?

University City Bank v. Brandel Center, Inc., et als.

Fred Strand planned the development of forty acres of land in Twin Falls, Idaho. The development was to include a shopping center, condominiums, an office building, and a hotel. Strand incorporated several entities, including defendant Brandel Center, Inc. ("BCI"), an Idaho corporation. Strand was the majority shareholder of BCI. BCI became the general partner of Brandel Gardens Hotel, Ltd. ("BGH"), a limited partnership formed to develop a hotel on the property. BCI owned one-half of BGH, while the other half was owned by approximately twenty limited partners, including George Matice and Matice Investment Company. BGH held title to the hotel built on the property, the Twin Falls Lodge and Conference Center, from the time that it was built until it was sold. Strand also formed Brandel Gardens Office Building ("BGOB") to develop the office building. That building, however, was never constructed.

Strand funded these ventures both through the sales of BCI shares and BGH limited partnerships, and through outside lenders, including a loan of $1.2 million from University City Bank, a Wyoming corporation. When this loan fell into default, University City Bank sued BCI, BGH and Strand in the appropriate United States District Court. The case was assigned to federal Judge Alton Davis. The case moved very slowly. Discovery was long and tedious and took over five years to complete. Several different attorneys moved into and out of the case. About two years ago, attorney Marlene Hazard joined the law firm representing BCI and assumed primary control over the case for all defendants. Although they knew about Ms. Hazard being in the case, and knew that she had been a law clerk to Judge Davis during the time the case was pending, the plaintiffs did not seek to recuse Judge Davis until about three weeks prior to trial. At that time, plaintiffs sought recusal of the judge and alleged in an affidavit that Ms. Hazard had served as law clerk for Judge Davis, that Ms. Hazard was responsible for this case while clerking for the judge. (You may assume these facts to be true). University City Bank now argues that §455 requires that Judge Davis self-disqualify.

Questions

1. Under §§144 and 455, is there a basis for disqualification of Judge Davis?
2. What is the best argument that can be made on behalf of the Strand/BCI/BGH?
3. Should Judge Davis be disqualified? Why or why not?

In re Federal Judges' Legislation

Upset by what it perceives as "activist" federal judges, the United States Congress adopted a statute providing that federal judges shall no longer have life tenure, but shall be subject to review by the Senate Judiciary Committee and possible reappointment every fifth year after their initial appointment. The Honorable Nanette Morgan is a federal district judge in the District of New Jersey. Upon signature of this bill by the President, Morgan filed suit in the United States District Court for the District of Columbia. She alleged that the statute violated the federal Constitution, specifically Article III, Section I. The case was assigned to United States District Court Judge Melinda Allenson pursuant to regular District of D.C. rules. Upon this assignment, however, the Department of Justice, on behalf of the United States, moved to disqualify Judge Allenson.

Questions

1. Does Judge Allenson, to whom this case is assigned, have an interest in the questioned legislation within the meaning of 28 U.S.C. §§144 and 455?
2. Is there any federal judge who does not have such an interest?
3. What should happen in such a case?

Jury Selection–Generally

Wastvan, et als v. Vail, et als.

The Farmers and Merchants National Bank of Hallsville is a small, suburban bank serving mostly farmers and other small business and residential customers in rural central Missouri.

The Bank was operated by a Board of Directors which included the following: Gilbert Wastvan a retired farmer; Ethel King, the wife of James King; Earl Lash, the President and CEO of the Bank; Aimee Lash, the sister of Earl Lash; Theodore House, a retired farmer; and Emily Hart, the wife of Nyland Hart, a deceased former director of the bank. All of the Directors were citizens of Missouri.

Some time ago, the Board of Directors received a Bank Examination Report from the United States Comptroller of the Currency. That report "expressed concern with the ratio of Bank capital to substandard loans, and what appears to be multiple violations of federal banking laws. The letter further warned of the potential "personal liability" of members of the board of directors who approved these loans.

Upon receipt of this letter, and the threat of personal liability, the Board hired David Vail of the law firm of Vail, Gillie & Foster, a Kansas professional corporation.

While it is unclear how the events transpired, eventually, the Comptroller assessed significant fines against the Bank and its Directors. After being assessed these fines, totaling more than $200,000 to each of them individually, the individual Directors filed a legal malpractice action against David Vail and his law firm. The suit claimed that Vail was hired by the individual Directors to prevent them from accruing personal liability. Vail, in defense, indicated that he was hired by the Bank, to defend the bank, and not by individuals.

The case is ready for trial in the United States District Court.

Question

All of the following have been called as prospective jurors in the case. Assess whether these prospective jurors should be excused for cause, excused by one of the parties using one of its peremptory challenges and whether any of them violated any laws in answering jury questionnaires:

Virginia Hilliard, is acquainted with the defendant, David Vail, because he has practiced in town for a number of years. She also knows of his firm and is familiar with the names of most of the members of that firm, although she probably cannot name any of them by name. She speaks to Mr. Vail when she meets him on the street, but she has never visited in his home and does not consider him a personal friend.

Vernon Long, is the owner of a gas station. His first wife was killed in an industrial accident. He did not sue anyone regarding this incident because the lawyer with whom he discussed the matter told him that the lawsuit would be very long and difficult and that he might not be able to emotionally withstand the difficulty and strain of the suit. He now knows he was wrong about not pursuing suit and upset at the lawyer with whom he discussed the case. He is considering a malpractice action against that lawyer, who is not a member of either the plaintiffs' or the defendants' law firm.

Gino Palletti, is a cook. He is somewhat ashamed of the fact that he can only write a few words in English, but that otherwise, he is unable to read or write the English language. He did not answer questions about reading and writing English on the jury questionnaire because he simply did not understand the questions.

Harriet Lange, is a schoolteacher in the Hallsville Public Schools. She has been told that the situation with the Farmers and Merchants Bank in Hallsville is "not good." She heard this from one of the other teachers at school who manages her teachers' union account that is on deposit in Farmers and Merchants Bank.

Rex Bullard, is a car dealer. Before taking that job, he was employed as an insurance adjuster with the Southland Casualty Company in Houston, Texas. He was fired from that job for processing false claims. He was prosecuted for and pleaded guilty to obtaining money under false pretenses which is a felony under Texas law. He received a suspended sentence. Because of that, he answered "no" on the jury questionnaire about criminal convictions.

Steve Lockwood is a telephone installer. He recalled reading articles in the newspaper about the Farmers and Merchants National Bank in Hallsville and about how the bank had some bad loans that it had provided to farmers in the area. He told his wife that the bank was pretty stupid for making such loans and that he would be upset if he were a depositor in the bank and were in danger of losing money as a result.

Sondra Lawson is the president and CEO of the Centralia Bank and Trust Company, a rival bank of Farmers and Merchants of Hallsville.

Marlyn Reyes is an Associate Professor at the local Law School. She teaches Property, Intellectual Property and Cyberspace Law. She is not a member of the state bar. She did, however, take and pass the Multistate Professional Responsibility Course and received law school training in both Professional Responsibility and Torts. She thus has a working knowledge of Legal Malpractice.

Elvira Clifford owns a restaurant/truck stop adjoining the Interstate. She does not know any of the parties or their attorneys. A friend of hers, however, was once represented by the defendant David Vail. She was not happy with the representation and blames Mr. Vail for losing.

Sebrina Hayes is a graduate student working on a PhD in Finance. Her thesis is on actions by the Comptroller of the Currency against rural banks that have made bad loans to farmers and the need of the United States to single out these banks as a strain on the Federal Reserve Bank.

Selecting a Jury–Batson Challenge

State v. Dixon

Dwayne Dixon was an African-American male. After Dwayne Dixon demanded money and/or drugs from Cornelius Dukes,   Dukes

walked into the bedroom of Dukes' apartment, retrieved a small amount
of crack cocaine, and gave it to Dixon.   Dixon was not satisfied and
demanded more drugs, and he and Dukes began scuffling.   Dixon
pointed a .39 revolver towards Dukes's abdomen, and witnesses heard
a gunshot as they saw the two men struggling.   Four more gunshots
later, Dukes lay dead. Dwayne Dixon was charged with murder. The
case proceeded to a jury trial.

Following voir dire questioning of perspective jurors, both sides
made peremptory strikes. Before the balance of the venire was excused
and the jury was sworn, both the State and Defendant raised *Batson*
challenges. Dixon's counsel challenged the State's peremptory strikes
of black venirepersons Shirley Alexander and Amazie McCain.   The
State challenged Defendant's peremptory strike of white venireperson
Mary Visintainer.

The prosecutor provided the following explanation for striking
Alexander:

> Your Honor, I struck her because she to me acted
> completely bored by the entire proceedings. I noticed
> once or twice her yawning. I noticed at least once when
> we took a brief, might have been a bench conference type
> of break or something and come back, that she actually,
> she rolled her eyes and looked disgusted that-because we
> were continuing on voir dire yesterday. And the same
> thing today, she looked pretty bored.   And I have
> nothing written down for her. I believe that she did not
> respond in terms of raising her hand to general
> questions but other than that did not participate in voir
> dire in any way.

In response to this explanation, defense counsel suggested that
the description of being "bored" and "tired" and concerned that the
process "was going on, on and on" applied to a lot of people.

The prosecutor provided the following explanation for striking
McCain:

> Your Honor, I struck her for basically the same reason
> as I struck [Alexander].   I-as I was speaking to
> everybody, I-I-frankly, I noticed the entire background
> there in the seats.   None of them appeared to be really
> particularly paying much attention. The two ladies, you
> know, I noticed them sort of exchanging glances
> occasionally. Again, like they were bored.   In terms of
> other people who were similarly situated, I would note
> that there were two other people. At least one of which
> stated on the record that she was bored. But those two
> people were struck for cause. If they weren't, I probably
> would have struck them peremptorily for the same
> reason. You know, if they couldn't give us a couple of
> hours of their time, you know, I don't think they would

make very good jurors for either side.

In response to this explanation, defense counsel noted that another white venireperson, Janice Rozmirsky, did not speak during his questioning and maybe answered a few of the prosecutor's questions, but she did not put forward "any great information."

The prosecutor replied to defense counsel's response by indicating that he did not get the same feeling from Rozmirsky anytime that he looked back at her. She was sitting over his shoulder so he did not observe her as much as the people in his line of sight. When he did turn around to look at the people behind him, Rozmirsky appeared to be alert, and he did not notice the same thing as in the others, "being bored."

Defense counsel provided the following explanation for striking Visintainer, a special education teacher:

> Actually, I wanted to keep [Visintainer]. The Defendant felt as though that would be a proper strike; I agree with him. I found it to be marginal except that my specific questioning as I relooked at her, my specific questioning with regard to learning disabilities and someone's-someone testifying. Although I think it was a point that could be made with everyone else, it could be a point that would actually offend her, that I'm addressing her students as being different or not being able to do certain things. It could also have created a reaction like well, by gosh my students would be able to come forward and testify if they were not guilty. So in retrospect, I agreed with my client.

In response to this explanation, the prosecutor stated that he did not "see any of that in terms of any responses that she had."

When the court found this explanation "speculative," defense counsel provided the following clarification of his explanation for his peremptory strike of Visintainer:

> I had placed her on my good list and it was my client who said that he had a feeling about her. And then in retrospect when I looked at her, I thought, well, considering the questioning that I did to her about her profession, I didn't see any problem. I didn't see her react that way. It was just simply the-the well, you never know. The way I addressed her with regard to her students and all of that on a very critical issue of the right not to testify, it was more of a-a-of my opportunity to have everyone else focus on those types of changes differences or–or difficulties but not to challenge [Visintainer] and her students. So upon my client's suggestion, I then thought well that might be a good choice. So just to make the record complete, I didn't think there was anything that anyone would have seen

and I didn't either, that made her-that seemed like she was offended.

Question

Discuss the validity of the peremptory challenges of Visintainer by the defense and McCain and Rozmirsky by the State.

Judgment as a Matter of Law

Before Submission to Jury

Caron v. AirFoods, Inc.

AirFood, Inc., a New York corporation, is engaged, nationwide, in the airline catering industry and prepares and supplies food to various airlines. AirFood's operations are based at various airports and are called Flight Kitchens. Andrea Caron is a citizen of New York who resigned from AirFood's Albany Flight Kitchen, claiming that she had been sexually harassed by John Tyren, the Kitchen's general manager. After following proper administrative procedure, she filed suit against both AirFood and Tyren, alleging sexual harassment and hostile work environment claims under federal statute and New York law. Tyren left AirFood's employment while Caron's suit was pending. Subsequently, AirFood rehired Caron to work in the Kitchen. At that time, AirFood was negotiating to sell the Kitchen to John Russo, the Kitchen's acting general manager. Russo and AirFood negotiated a sale whereby AirFood agreed to transfer the Kitchen to Russo's company, Air Catering, Inc., another New York corporation. Because, under the sale agreement, Russo was prohibited from using AirFood's prior computer system, Russo needed to hire someone to develop a computer software billing and accounting system. Russo hired John Tyren as a consultant because of his past experience with the airline catering industry. This position necessitated Tyren's presence at the Kitchen. Upset by Tyren's presence at the Kitchen, Caron took an approved vacation until Tyren finished his consulting work. Shortly after returning to work, Caron was deposed in connection with her lawsuit. Tyren was present during the deposition and told Russo about Caron's testimony. Three days later, Russo told Caron that he would not keep her on as an employee with Ground-to-Air Catering.

Caron filed an amended complaint, adding a cause of action for retaliation against AirFood on the alleged bases that it discharged her and refused to transfer her in retaliation for her deposition testimony. She did not add Russo or Air Catering as a party. You should assume for the purpose of this problem that both federal and New York law prohibits an employer from discriminating against an employee who files or testifies in any type of Human Rights claim. To be successful, however, the employee must show that it was actually "their employer," not some other party, who did the discriminatory act.

Caron proceeded with her retaliation claim against AirFood on two alternative bases: (1) AirFood wrongfully discharged her or (2) AirFood wrongfully failed to transfer her to another job in retaliation for her deposition testimony.

Following discover in the case, AirFood, Inc. moved for Summary Judgment on all claims by Andrea Caron. The trial court denied that motion.

Caron's testimony revealed that on the last day she worked for AirFood, James Russo informed her that "he wasn't gonna keep [her] on" and that she "wouldn't have a job with his new company"). The testimony also revealed that AirFood sold the Kitchen to Air Catering. A representative of AirFood testified that Caron did not request a transfer prior to the sale and Caron, in her deposition, agreed with this testimony. The personnel manager of AirFood also testified that Caron was treated the same as other Kitchen employees who were not retained by Air Catering.

At the conclusion of all of the evidence, AirFood, Inc. moved for Judgment as a Matter of Law.

Questions

1. Caron argues that, having denied Summary Judgment to AirFood, Inc. following discovery, the court cannot now grant Judgment as a Matter of Law? Is she right? Why or why not? What are the similarities between Summary Judgment and Judgment as a Matter of Law?

2. How should the court rule on AirFood's motion? Why?

Judgment as a Matter of Law and Motion for New Trial

Zenk v. Home Rite Company

Firefighters arrived at the home of Laurie Zenk to discover flames around the front entrance. Upon entering the home, they found Zenk in an upstairs bathroom, dead of carbon monoxide poisoning. At the time of her death, Laurie Zenk was a citizen of Illinois. Her son, petitioner Chad Zenk, individually and on behalf of Laurie Zenk's heirs, brought a diversity action in the United States District Court for the District of North Dakota seeking wrongful death damages. He alleged that a defect in an electric baseboard heater, manufactured by defendant Home Rite Company and located inside the door to Laurie Zenk's home, caused both the fire and his mother's death. Home Rite Company is a corporate citizen of North Dakota.

At trial, Zenk introduced the testimony of three witnesses, proffered as experts, in an endeavor to prove the alleged defect in the heater and its causal connection to the fire. The District Court overruled defendant Home Rite's objections, lodged both before and during the trial, that this testimony was unreliable and therefore was not admissible under various Supreme Court cases. At the close of Zenk's evidence, and again at the close of all the evidence, Home Rite unsuccessfully moved under Rule 50(a) for judgment as a matter of law on the ground that Zenk had failed to meet his burden of proof on the issues of defect and causation. The jury returned a verdict for Zenk. Home Rite again requested judgment as a matter of law, and additionally requested, in the alternative, a new trial, pursuant to Rules 50 and 59; among arguments in support of its post-trial motions, Home Rite reasserted that the expert testimony essential to prove Zenk's case was unreliable and therefore inadmissible. The District Court denied the motions and entered judgment for Zenk. Home Rite appealed.

The Court of Appeals held that Home Rite's motion for judgment as a matter of law should have been granted. The court of appeals first examined the testimony of Zenk's expert witnesses, the sole evidence supporting plaintiffs' product defect charge. Concluding that the testimony was speculative and not shown to be scientifically sound, the majority held the expert evidence incompetent to prove Zenk's case. The court then considered Zenk's request for a new trial. In doing so, the court considered the remaining evidence in the light most favorable to Zenk, found it insufficient to support the jury verdict, and directed judgment as a matter of law for Home Rite.

Questions

1. Assess the conduct of Home Rite. Did Home Rite's attorneys move for judgment as a matter of law at the correct times during the trial? Why or why not?

2. Following the trial, Home Rite again moved for judgment as a matter of law. What gives Home Rite the right to do that? Why might a judge be more inclined to grant this motion then the same judge would have been prior to the jury verdict?

3. Following the trial, Home Rite combined the motion for a judgment as a matter of law with a motion for new trial. Why? What is the difference?

4. The problem does not say, but following trial, when did the motion for judgment as a matter of law and/or motion for new trial need to be filed?

5. Under Rule 50, Zenk wants to argue to the United States

Supreme Court that when a court of appeals determines that a jury verdict cannot be sustained due to an error in the admission of evidence, the appellate court may not order the entry of judgment for the verdict loser, but must instead remand the case to the trial court for a new trial determination. Is this what Rule 50 requires in this circumstance?

New Trial

Newly Discovered Evidence

Defenders of Nature, Inc. v. Central School District

The facts for this problem are set out earlier in this Chapter. Recall that expert witness Mary Daniels indicated that after she initially went to the proposed school site and determined that no pygmy-owls had been in residence, she returned to the site the following day to verify that she had in fact seen an elf owl rather than a pygmy-owl because distinguishing between the two is often difficult. She verified that she did see an elf owl. Also assume that Defenders' expert, Max Alton, surprised at Mary Daniels' testimony, returned to the site the day following the hearing. He discovered physical evidence, such as old owl pelts, dried lizard remains, lice, and nesting material in one of the saguaros, which could indicate that a pygmy-owl had previously nested near the center of the property.

Question

Assume that a court would admit the Max Alton observations. Are they new? Do they constitute "newly discovered evidence?" Why or why not?

Conduct of the Court

Hawk v. Wagner, et als

Jeffrey S. Hawk filed a civil lawsuit in the proper federal district court alleging both federal and state claims arising from an incident during his intake at the Travis County Jail after his arrest on an assault charge. Hawk alleged that, while shackled, he was grabbed in a headlock, attacked by several jail officers, and dropped to the floor. As the result of this incident, Hawk alleged that he suffered a broken jaw and loosened or broken teeth. The incident was recorded on videotape, with audio, and the tape was introduced into evidence at the trial.

Hawk named as defendants in his lawsuit Travis County corrections officer Todd Wagner, the Sheriff of Travis County, and several other city, county and state officials. Hawk's federal claims, brought pursuant to 42 U.S.C. §§ 1983 and 1985, alleged deprivation of Hawk's constitutional rights and conspiracy to deprive him of his constitutional rights premised on use of excessive force. Hawk's state common-law claims alleged assault and battery, intentional infliction of emotional distress, negligent infliction of emotional distress, "negligence," "recklessness," and "respondeat superior."

The case was tried to a jury, which returned a verdict in favor of Hawk and against Officer Wagner. However, the jury found in favor of the remaining defendants. The jury awarded damages against Officer Wagner in the amount of approximately $64,700.

Officer Wagner now moves for a new trial.

Questions

1. Officer Wagner premises the motion for new trial, in part, on actions of the trial judge during the trial. Consider whether each of the following justifies the granting of a new trial. Also consider whether the totality of all the following justifies such a grant:

    A. Following the trial, the trial judge had an in chambers meeting with, among others, Wagner's counsel. This meeting was about the trial schedule in another case. The meeting was tape recorded, as was the judge's custom. The transcription of the judge's comments provided by defense counsel reads as follows:

> I think last week you thought you were getting picked on and maybe you were a little bit, although I hope not, but that's a kind of a gross situation. I realize you and your expert gotta look at that in the best light, but I come pretty damn close to asking the U.S. Attorney to charge those police officers with civil rights criminal violations. I might yet. That's gross, and you can put all the spin on it you want, but when you try to tell me that when the guy is down, they got his head, they got his hands behind his back, he's got one leg on the floor so he can [sic] kick, and then somehow he kicks, so his leg is up here, and that's that wild kick that they're all so afraid of. It's absolutely impossible, unless somebody knocks his other leg out. I don't care who you are. I probably shouldn't be talking, but the point is, those guys, if there wasn't any videotape, I really would hate to hear what story those guys had. We had--the last time we had a videotape, the officers--the defendants didn't know it. Were you in that case? They all told bald-faced lies. After they all told their lies, then the videotape came out, just exactly the opposite of what

they said, so I think that Travis County police aren't any better than the guys who'd beaten those Mexicans out on the road and they aren't any better than Rodney King's guys, and if your clients and you don't think so, you've been trying too many of these cases. God bless you.

When reviewing post trial comments by the judge, how can those comments become grounds for a new trial? Do these comments justify a new trial? Why or why not?

      B. During the trial, Mr. Wagner produced an expert witness. The witness testified at the end of one trial day and the beginning of the next. At the start of cross examination of the expert on the second day, Mr. Hawk's counsel, Mr. Pennington, discussed the expert's testimony that the videotape of the incident could have been "manipulated." The testimony was as follows:

Q [BY MR. Taney]: And as a result of this manipulation, as you call it, by the attorneys, I guess you had to do a little damage control and work with Mr. Wagner last night, didn't you?

A [BY MR. BOLTON, DEFENDANTS' EXPERT]: Nope.

 I just tried to explain to him that he should testify to the truth, that he should understand the questions before he answers, and that if the attorney tries to trip him up, make him qualify the--the question.

Q: He wasn't telling--he didn't know to tell the truth yesterday without your advice, Mr. Bolton?

A: Oh, I'm sure he did.

Q: Well, Mr. Bolton, isn't it a fair statement that in a case like this, we don't need your expert testimony or even our expert testimony when there is a videotape of the entire incident, isn't that the best evidence, Mr. Bolton?

A: Coming from you, counselor, I don't know what a fair statement is.

THE COURT: Just a minute, now.

MR. Taney: Your Honor--

THE COURT: You answer his questions. If you have something you want to say later, Mr. Phillips will ask you about it, but we don't need your comments and your criticism. You just answer the questions.

THE WITNESS: Yes, sir.

Mr. Wagner now argues that this open hostility towards the witness by the court justifies a new trial on two basis: First, it suggests to the jury that the witness was lying; Second, the trial judge did not have a similar interchange with one of Hawk's expert witnesses. Should this exchange justify a new trial? Why or why not?

      C. During the trial, on cross examination of Hawk, Wagner's counsel asked: "Isn't it true that you threatened to sue the

officers within a matter of seconds after you hit the floor?"   Although
there was no objection to the question from plaintiff's counsel, the trial
judge stopped the proceedings, excused the jury, and during the recess
met with counsel in chambers to review the videotape, because the trial
judge recalled hearing no such comments on the tape. Upon a return to
open court, the trial judge gave the following instruction, which defense
counsel asserts was unnecessary and unfairly prejudicial to the
defendants:

> THE COURT: Please be seated. Members of the jury,
> I was listening to the matters as we went along here,
> and I came upon a situation that I was not fully
> cognizant of, and so I stopped and I wanted to go back
> and I wanted to listen to this tape, and especially the
> audio part of it. Remember, I am not a witness, but I
> had to watch and listen to this tape five or six or seven
> or eight times, and I hadn't heard that. So I sent you
> downstairs, and we listened carefully to this tape. At
> 2:34:20 on the tape, these words, and they're hard to
> hear--I don't know whether you heard them when it's
> been played to you before or not--but the words are
> these: "If you don't send me to the hospital, I'm going to
> sue you." And this was six and a half minutes after he
> hit the floor, and that's at 2:27:51 when he hit the floor.
> I felt that you should have that accurately brought
> before you.   I'm going to ask you to--direct you to
> disregard any other question about any other time. All
> right. Now, let's go back. Counsel for Mr. Wagner was
> on cross-examination and you may proceed.

Does this statement by the trial court justify a new trial? Why
or why not?

      D. Because the case rested, according to the judge,
"substantially on the videotape," the court limited both the defendants
and the plaintiff to 10 hours each of trial time. Wagner argues that such
a limitation compels a new trial. Is this correct? Why or why not?

      E. Do all four of these actions, in their totality, justify a
new trial? Why or why not?

      2. Suppose, in considering the record, the trial judge says to
herself: "If I were sitting on the jury, I would not have reached this
verdict." Should the trial judge grant a motion for new trial? Why or
why not?

      3. Assume that on the day set for closing arguments, plaintiff's
counsel opened the remarks and was followed by defense counsel,
followed by plaintiff's counsel on rebuttal. As the jury was exiting the
courtroom, immediately after plaintiff's counsel had ended closing
arguments, defendant Wagner suffered a panic attack, during which he
began to scream in a very high pitched loud voice and then collapsed on
the floor of the courtroom. Immediately after this incident, the court in

chambers and on the record interrogated the Court Officer escorting the jury. That officer swore, under oath that the last juror leaving the courtroom saw the outburst. The Officer stated that he was not sure about how many jurors had left the courtroom or had gone beyond the courtroom door. "I'm not sure about that. I was holding the door when the last one passed and I heard the noise. I asked what is that.... The last [juror] said Officer Wagner fell down." When asked if the other jurors were close to him, the Court Officer replied: "Very close. When I heard the noise, I started pushing the people, the jurors into the jury room. When I got them there, I heard them making comments inside the jury room about the incident." There is no question but that the panic attack of Officer Wagner was genuine. Should the court grant a new trial? Why or why not?

Remittitur

Restin, et al. v. HealthFirst Foundation, Inc.

Margaret Restin and Dana Metzger filed claims of race discrimination in connection with the termination of their employment as licensed practical nurses (LPNs) from the Downtown Health Care Center, a nursing home facility owned and operated by HealthFirst Foundation, Inc. The trial was bifurcated and the jury first found that HealthFirst Foundation did discriminate against both Ms. Restin and Ms. Metzger. The case then proceeded to a hearing regarding damages of both plaintiffs.

At the damage hearing, Ms. Restin testified that as a result of being fired on December 19--one week before Christmas--she suffered the embarrassment, humiliation, emotional pain, and mental anguish of telling her three children that there would be no Christmas in the Restin home. She also had to tell her daughter, a high school senior, that there was no money for her daughter's once-in-a-lifetime senior class trip, that she could not financially help her daughter fulfill her dream of going to college, and that because she could get no credit after losing her job, her daughter's student loan would not go through. Ms. Restin suffered embarrassment and humiliation at work when wrongfully accused of patient neglect. Physically, Ms. Restin experienced stress, headaches, sleeplessness, and an upset stomach. She has not seen a doctor or other health care professional because she had no money and no health insurance, and she had to feed, clothe, and raise her children with what she did have. Ms. Restin testified that she suffered emotional distress from being unemployed and that the loss of her job destroyed her financially--her car was repossessed, she was sued by her creditors, her wages have been garnished, she lost (and still cannot get today) credit cards or credit at any stores. Ms. Restin also testified that she had been unemployed for about two years before working for Downtown Health and that she was terminated from her last job before working at Downtown Health.

Ms. Metzger testified that because of her color she was forced to resign her position as unit director; she did not receive the same wages as her peers; she was required to attend a meeting with her peers in which her performance was discussed and she was ridiculed and embarrassed; she was repeatedly told that positions for LPNs were not available on the medical specialty unit even though less experienced white LPNs were given jobs there; she was subjected to intense scrutiny and was called into the administrator's office to explain her action after filing a charge of discrimination; she was selected for layoff when a less senior white LPN retained her position; she was toyed with and lied to regarding a bogus return-to-work call after her layoff.

Based largely on this testimony, the jury awarded Ms. Restin $20,000 in back pay and benefits, and $150,000 in compensatory damages. The jury awarded Ms. Metzger $14,783.05 in back pay and benefits, and $100,000 in compensatory damages.

Pursuant to Rule 59, the defendants moved for a new trial with regard to damages or alternatively to alter the jury's verdict by reducing the damages awarded. The trial court determined that there was no justification for a new trial but was willing to consider whether damages should be reduced.

Questions

1. What factors should the court consider in determining whether damages should be reduced?

2. Should the court consider what has happened in other cases in ruling on the amount of damages? Aren't damages uniquely personal?

3. If the court believed that the damage award was too high, how would it construct an order calling for Remittitur?

4. Suppose that the plaintiffs wanted to argue the damages were too low. Can they ask for additur? Why or why not?

CHAPTER 10

DEALING WITH JUDGMENTS

Claim Preclusion Basics

Dorchard & Gebhard v. Acorn County School District

Janet Dorchard and Maria Gebhard were both high school teachers employed by the Acorn County School District in central Iowa. Pursuant to state law, Acorn County Superintendent of Schools Alexander Rollins notified both Dorchard and Gebhard that their teaching contracts were not being renewed. In his letter, Superintendent Rollins listed the reasons for nonrenewal as follows:

1. Conversion of school property;
2. Misappropriation of school property.
3. Poor role model.
4. Unprofessional conduct.
5. Inappropriate student supervision.
6. Retaliation against students and staff.
7. Inappropriate student discipline.

Dorchard and Gebhard both contested their nonrenewal and, pursuant to state law and their teacher contract, the Acorn County School District held a hearing on the matter. The hearing took nine days, the school district and both Dorchard and Gebhard were represented by counsel and considerable evidence was heard. At the conclusion of the hearing, the School District Board issued a 32 page report on each of the two teachers finding that just cause existed for termination of Dorchard and Gebhard's contract based on the seven reasons listed in the Superintendent's letter. Dorchard and Gebhard then filed an action in state court challenging their administrative dismissal. Under state law, the state trial court shall reverse, modify, or grant any other appropriate relief from the Boar d decision or the adjudicator's decision equitable or legal and including declaratory relief if substantial rights of the petitioner have been prejudiced because the action is: (1) in violation of constitutional or statutory provisions; ... or (4) made upon unlawful procedure; or (5) affected by other error of law; ... or (7) unreasonable, arbitrary, or capricious or characterized by an abuse of discretion. The state trial court upheld the dismissals and these terminations were upheld on appeal through the state court.

Dorchard and Gebhard then filed a charge of sex discrimination with the United States Equal Opportunity Employment Commission alleging violations of Title VII of the federal Civil Rights Act of 1964. As a result, they received from the EEOC a Notice of Right to Sue. They then filed an action in the United States District Court for the Central District of Iowa against the Acorn County District School Board alleging that they were discharged based on illegal sex discrimination in violation of Title VII of the federal Civil Rights act.

Questions

1. If the School Board denies discrimination, can it later raise claim preclusion at trial?
2. Where will the federal court look to determine what is the law of preclusion applicable to the case?
3. Assuming that the School Board pleads preclusion as an affirmative defense, and then moves for Summary Judgment, how should the court rule? Why?

Claim Preclusion--Identical Claims

International Discounters, Inc. v. Linden

International Discounters, Inc. is a corporate citizen of Nevada. Known in internet circles as IDI, International Discounters, Inc. is a discount buying club. For a membership fee of $149.99, payable in four convenient monthly installments of $37.50 each, members can take advantage of the buying power possessed by literally millions of consumers on items from anchors to zincographs. Murphy and Eunice Linden are husband and wife and are citizens of Mississippi. Several years ago, the Lindens purchased membership in the IDI Buying Club. Unhappy with the discounts they were receiving on various items, the Lindens sued IDI in a United States District Court in Nevada alleging breach of the discount buying contract between the parties. The Lindens claimed that they had plans to purchase at least $80,000 worth of consumer goods over the course of the agreement and were prevented from so doing by policies in force in the agreement. The Lindens created a website that generally disparaged IDI and spent a great deal of time and energy trying to publicly humiliate the company. International Discounters, Inc. defended the Linden's lawsuit, moved for summary judgment and filed a motion under Rule 11 alleging that the prosecution of the suit was frivolous and being presented only for the purpose of harassment of IDI. The trial court granted summary judgment in favor of IDI, dismissed the suit by the Lindens, but denied any relief under Rule 11.

Thereafter, International Discounters, Inc., which claims to have lost substantial money as a result of the Lindens claim, filed suit against the Lindens in the United States District Court in Mississippi. That suit claims the Lindens are liable to IDI under the tort of Malicious Prosecution. For purpose of this problem, you may assume that the elements of that tort, under Mississippi state law are: (1) a judicial proceeding initiated by the defendant; (2) the lack of probable cause; (3) malice on the part of the defendant; (4) termination of the judicial proceeding favorably to the plaintiff; and, (5) damages. Counsel for the Lindens have moved for summary judgment alleging that the malicious prosecution proceeding is barred either by the compulsory counterclaim provisions of Rule 13(a) or by claim preclusion.

Questions

1. Is the subsequent claim barred by Rule 13(a)? Why or why not?

2. Is the subsequent claim barred by claim preclusion? Why or why not?

Marchand v. National Health Association

Valerie Marchand, an African American female was fired from her job as a consultant at National Health Association, Inc. She filed suit over her termination in the federal court alleging that her termination was the result of illegal discrimination and retaliation based on race, sex and age, all in violation of federal law. The complaint alleged that Marchand was denied promotion and subjected to a hostile work environment, and further alleged that the discriminatory treatment caused her private physician to place her on "sickness disability" for thirty days. The relief demanded by Marchand included long-term disability benefit pay. This claim was filed in a proper United States District Court. Throughout this proceeding, National Health told Valerie that they wanted her to return to her original position after the proceeding was over. At the conclusion of a bench trial, the trial court granted National Health Association's motion for summary judgment on this claim. Following the termination of this lawsuit, National Health again asked Marchand to return to her original job and she continued to work for National Health until she was later terminated.

Valerie Marchand then filed a second lawsuit. That suit alleged that National Health failed to accommodate a disability of Marchand when it continued to require her to perform her regular duties and did not reassign her to a different position when her private physician placed her on "sickness disability" and that National Health wrongfully terminated her, both claims again in violation of federal law. National Health Association has moved to dismiss the second claim on the basis of claim preclusion.

Question

What result on National Health's motion? Why?

Claim Preclusion–Identical Claim–Compulsory Counterclaim Rule

Griffin Fitzwater, et als. v. Ernest Blackwell, Alfred Camp, Garrett Randall, et als.

Third Missionary Baptist Church of Pageland, South Carolina, is a South Carolina corporation and a congregational, self-governing, autonomous organization. The Church is governed only by its articles of incorporation and the Bible's New Testament. The pastor is the moderator of all meetings, and the will of the membership controls on all issues of governance. Under the church's bylaws, the 'right hand of fellowship', with all privileges as voting members, is accorded every person when baptized, children included.

Ernest Blackwell, Alfred Camp, and Garrett Randall are all citizens of Monroe, North Carolina. They are all adults and baptized members of Third Missionary Baptist Church, which, although in a different state, is just down the road from their homes.

Apparently because of some internal church crisis not relevant here, issues were presented Third Missionary's Pastor Bell, who raised them at the congregation's quarterly meeting in April, two years ago. As a result of this discussion, Pastor Bell purged the church's rolls of all parishioners under 21 years of age and any who had not communed for the prior three months. Confusion resulted and the session adjourned.

Prior to the next scheduled congregational meeting in June, two years ago, advance publication of an agenda for that meeting was made at two prior Sunday services. Shortly after this June meeting convened, a request was made for a vote to determine whether Pastor Bell should be retained. There was confusion. Pastor Bell tried to adjourn the meeting. One of the parishioners present, however, immediately asked those in attendance to remain so there could be a vote on retention of the minister. Some people walked out but about 75 or 80 remained. Pastor Bell's wife started playing a piano and he began singing, in an attempt to interrupt proceedings. However, as best as could be determined, a majority of those present voted to remove Pastor Bell from the pastorate. In addition, Ernest Blackwell and Alfred Camp, both of whom were church trustees, and Garrett Randall, who was the church's treasurer, were unanimously voted out of office. They were replaced by Griffin Fitzwater and two others.

Evidently undaunted, Ernest Blackwell, Alfred Camp, Garrett Randall and Pastor Bell, unable to gain access to the church building, met in Randall's backyard with several other parishioners. They voted the Fitzwater group out of office and reinstated themselves.

Thereafter, Blackwell, Camp, and Randall filed an action in South Carolina state court seeking a temporary injunction to restrain what they referred to as "the bogus new board (Fitzwater, et als) from dealing with property of the church. The defendants in that action, including Griffin Fitzwater, counterclaimed seeking an accounting by the Blackwell group of all assets of the parish.

The trial court in the South Carolina matter, upon motion by the defendants, held the matters involved were ecclesiastical and that, as a result, the trial court had no jurisdiction. The court dissolved a temporary injunction previously issued and entered an Order of dismissal. No appeal was taken.

Thereafter, Griffin Fitzwater and others filed a suit in the federal court in North Carolina against Blackwell, Camp, and Randall, seeking an accounting of all assets of the parish and alleging that Blackwater, Camp, Randall, Pastor Bell and others were in control of these assets, having refused to surrender them following the initial election voted these parishioners out of office. It was estimated that the parish owned about $350,000 worth of assets.

Attorneys for Blackwell, Camp, and Randall have moved to dismiss alleging both that the current claim is barred by the compulsory counterclaim rule and that it is barred by claim preclusion.

Questions

1. Will claim preclusion bar the second suit? Why or why not?
2. Will the compulsory counterclaim rule bar the second suit? Why or why not?

Claim Preclusion--Identical Parties

Preston v. Arkin and Wilhelm

Capital Mortgage Services, Inc. is a corporate citizen of New Mexico and was represented by the law firm of Arkin and Wilhelm, all of whose partners were citizens of New Mexico. On behalf of Capital, Arkin and Wilhelm attorneys filed a mortgage foreclosure action against Diane Preston, a citizen of Arizona, after a note in the amount of $500,000 that Capital Mortgage secured had become delinquent. Diane Preston filed an answer that admitted the delinquency, but asserted a counterclaim based upon a federal claim of common law lien. The counterclaim asserted that the common-law lien was paramount and superior to Capital's mortgage. As it turned out, the law disagreed with Preston's assertion and despite her attorney's vigorous assertion of this defense, the trial court granted summary judgment against Preston on her counterclaim and in favor of Capital Mortgage Services on its foreclosure claim.

The terms of her note and mortgage obligated Preston to pay Capital Mortgage's "reasonable attorney's fees" in the event of a default. As a result, as part of the foreclosure proceeding, Arkin and Wilhelm submitted affidavits showing an entitlement to $80,000 in attorney's fees, part of which were due to the "novel" counterclaim interposed by Preston. Preston, through her attorney, protested the amount of these attorneys' fees, but eventually stipulated to their reasonableness and did not challenge them in the foreclosure action. The amount of the attorney's fees were included in the foreclosure judgment.

After the foreclosure action was concluded, Diane Preston filed suit in the appropriate United States District Court against Arkin and Wilhelm challenging the reasonableness of the fees awarded the law firm in the foreclosure action.

Question

Arkin and Wilhelm move to dismiss Diane Preston's federal complaint, alleging that Preston's claim is precluded. Preston argues that the parties to the second proceeding are different and that claim preclusion does not, therefore, apply. What result? Why?

Claim Preclusion--Identical Parties/Identical Claims

Valley v. Material Transport, et als.

Darrin S. Valley is a citizen of Georgia and owns a car. While traveling on U.S. Highway 1, near its intersection with U.S. Highway 341 in Baxley, Valley's car was struck by two semi-trucks. The first of those was owned by Material Transport, Inc., a corporate citizen of Delaware and driven by Harvey Green, an employee of Material Transport and a citizen of Maryland. The other truck was owned by Lagos, Inc., a corporate citizen of Delaware and driven by Amber Law, an employee of Lagos and a citizen of North Carolina. In the accident, both the Material Transport truck driven by Green and the Lagos, Inc. truck driven by Law were proceeding in the same direction on the multi-lane highway 341. Both approached a red light at the signal-controlled intersection and both apparently ignored the red light. Darrin Valley was driving his vehicle and approached the intersection on the multi-lane highway 1. Because the light was green for his lane of traffic, Valley entered the intersection. The front of his vehicle was struck by the Material Transport vehicle and the rear of his vehicle was struck by the Lagos truck. Valley sustained severe injuries.

Questions

1. Darrin Valley filed suit against Harvey Green, alleging that Green negligently drove the Material Transport truck and that he did so while in the lawful performance of his duties as an employee of Material Transport. In a trial before the judge, the court found that Green was not negligent. Darrin Valley then filed suit against Material Transport alleging that it was liable under the doctrine of Respondeat Superior as the employer of Harvey Green. Darrin Valley says this claim is permissible because the parties are different. Is this claim precluded? Why or why not?

2. Assume instead that Darrin Valley filed suit against Amber Law, alleging that Law negligently drove the Lagos, Inc. truck and that she did so while in the lawful performance of her duties as an employee of Lagos, Inc. In a trial before the judge, the court found that Law was not negligent. Darrin Law then filed suit against Lagos, Inc. alleging that Lagos negligently entrusted the truck to Amber Law. As it turns out, Amber Law's operator's license had been suspended six months before this incident and this fact could have been known by Lagos, Inc.'s personnel department. Is this claim precluded? Why or why not?

3. Assume instead that Darrin Valley filed suit against Amber Law, alleging that Law negligently drove the Lagos, Inc. truck and that she did so while in the lawful performance of her duties as an employee

of Lagos, Inc. The case was tried to a jury which returned a general verdict for Law. Darrin Valley then filed suit against Lagos, Inc. alleging that it was liable under the doctrine of Respondeat Superior as the employer of Amber Law. How is the preclusion issue in this question different from the one you answered in Question 1. What result on this question? Why?

Issue Preclusion–Identity of Issues

Bennett v. James

Luther James, a citizen of Minnesota, was something of a career criminal. Arlene Bennett, a citizen of Illinois, was a federal border patrol agent stationed at the Canadian border in Minnesota. When Bennett stopped a car being driven by James as it was reentering the United States, she noticed what appeared to be plants sticking out from under a jacket on the back seat. When she asked James about it, James tried to drive away, but was unable to do so. Arlene Bennett drew her weapon and fired several times at the back of the James vehicle in an attempt to stop the car. James could not get away and, in an apparent attempt to stop Bennett shooting at him, James put his car in reverse and started to back straight into Bennett. Bennett fired several more shots at James' vehicle, but it did not stop, and Bennett had to jump out of the vehicle's path to avoid being hit. Bennett fell to the ground and sustained severe and permanent injuries.

James was charged under federal law with possession of a controlled substance, marijuana, and with assault on a federal officer. At trial, in charging the jury, the judge instructed that "a person commits the crime of assault upon a federal officer in the second degree when the person `attempts to cause physical injury to a federal officer by means of a deadly weapon or dangerous instrument'." A federal jury convicted James on both charges.

Arlene Bennett and her husband also sued James for the intentional tort of assault in the appropriate federal court. Bennett and her husband moved for summary judgment claiming that issue preclusion barred James from relitigating the issue of whether he assaulted Bennett. Luther James contends that issue preclusion does not apply in this case because the issue of intent was not specifically determined in the criminal case. Thus, he argues, the issues are not identical, he did not have an opportunity to litigate the issue in the prior case and precluding re-litigation of the issue would be inequitable.

Question

How should the court rule? Why? Is there additional information you need? What is it?

Lentz v. Westman Corporation

This problem presents a state case. You should assume, regardless of what you might know about this state's law, that the state follows a view of preclusion that would be followed by the federal courts in that state.

The Ohio State Treasurer is the custodian of the Second Injury Fund ("SIF"). The second injury fund is part of the state's Worker Compensation system. It pays injured employees after a work injury "combines with a prior disability to create an increased combined disability."

A year or so ago, Ronnie Lentz filed a Claim for Compensation against his employer Westman Corporation and the Second Injury Fund ("SIF") based on a repetitive motion injury sustained while working on an assembly line. For reasons not pertinent to this problem, the Administrative Law Judge assigned this case bifurcated the matter. The judge scheduled and held a hearing of Lentz's claim against Westman for temporary total disability (TTD) and permanent partial disability (PPD) benefits and entered a Judgment for Benefits in favor of Lentz on those claims.

Following resolution of the temporary and permanent partial disability ("PPD") claims against Westman, an Administrative Law Judge ("ALJ") scheduled a hearing to resolve the Claim for permanent total disability (PTD) benefits against the SIF. Lawyers for the SIF objected and moved to dismiss any remaining claims based upon issue preclusion.

Questions

1. Without worrying about the actual requirements of the law, what facts do you believe Lentz must show to prove entitlement to Temporary Total Disability?

2. Without worrying about the actual requirements of the law, what facts do you believe Lentz must show to prove entitlement to Permanent Partial Disability?

3. Without worrying about the actual requirements of the law, what facts do you believe Lentz must show to prove entitlement to Permanent Total Disability?

4. What result on this motion? Why?

Offensive Use of Issue Preclusion

Grubman v. District of Columbia

In 1934, following the repeal of Prohibition, Congress enacted the ABC Act to regulate the importation and distribution of liquor within the District of Columbia.

In addition, the ABC Act authorized the Council of the District of Columbia to adopt rules to "control and regulate the manufacture, sale, keeping for sale, offer for sale, solicitation of orders for sale, importation, exportation, and transportation of alcoholic beverages in the District of Columbia." Acting pursuant to this provision, the Council enacted the District of Columbia Wholesale Liquor Industry Storage Act. The act required that no wholesaler licensed by the District shall "store beverages upon premises outside the District."

Grubman & Co., Inc., is a D.C. based wholesaler of alcoholic beverages licensed under the ABC Act, distributing liquor, beer and wine to District of Columbia retailers. Grubman is authorized to store alcoholic beverages at two locations within the District. A Maryland affiliate of Grubman, The J.G Company, Inc., is a licensed wholesale distributor of alcoholic beverages in Maryland. Grubman desired to consolidate its warehousing operations in the District and Maryland by leasing a facility in Jessup, Maryland. Toward this end, Grubman filed suit in district court seeking to enjoin enforcement of the Storage Act alleging that the act was unconstitutional. Grubman moved for summary judgment on the issue of the Constitutionality of the Storage Act, arguing that the earlier district court decision in *Quality Brands, Inc. v. Barry*, 715 F.Supp. 1138 (D.D.C.1989) had resolved the question. In that case, Quality Brands, Inc., a licensed alcoholic beverage wholesaler in the District and a competitor of Grubman, sought a declaratory judgment that the Storage Act was unconstitutional. The district court held that (1) the local warehousing requirement facially discriminated against interstate commerce in violation of the Commerce Clause, (2) the articulated purposes given for the requirement could not withstand the "strict scrutiny" accorded facially discriminatory legislation, and (3) the Twenty-first Amendment did not shield the District's discrimination against interstate commerce, Consequently, the *Quality Brands* court concluded that the local warehousing requirement violated the Commerce Clause and enjoined its enforcement. The District of Columbia appealed the trial court's decision and the Court of Appeals summarily affirmed the decision, without opinion.

Grubman argues that because the District actually litigated the Constitutionality of the Storage Act in *Quality Brands,* and because there was a decision by a court of competent jurisdiction, it would not be unfair to apply the decision against the District now. Accordingly,

Grubman wants to apply "Offensive" issue preclusion to resolve the Constitutionality issue.

Question

What result? Why?

Defensive Use of Issue Preclusion

Owens v. Woodbury County

For fourteen years Darby Owens served as a deputy sheriff in Woodbury County, Connecticut. When Darby Owens resigned, the sheriff was Tory Huntsman. Approximately two years prior to his resignation, Darby Owens was divorced by his wife and he was ordered to pay child support. At about the same time, or immediately thereafter, a female friend of Darby Owens filed criminal complaints against him because of a personal dispute. Because they involved a member of his department, Sheriff Huntsman referred these complaints to the Connecticut Division of Criminal Investigation (DCI). After the DCI had completed its investigation, it filed five criminal charges against Darby Owens. These charges were in no way related to the criminal complaints filed by Darby Owens's female friend. Subsequently, the state court dismissed the criminal charges and its dismissal was affirmed on appeal by the state supreme court.

While the criminal charges were pending, Tory Huntsman placed Darby Owens on a paid suspension and prohibited him from engaging in any off-duty law enforcement work. After Darby Owens had been on a paid suspension for eighteen months and while his appeal was still pending before the state supreme court, Tory Huntsman allowed him to return to work, provided that Darby Owens would agree to a thirty-day unpaid suspension and enter into a "Last Chance Agreement." The agreement provided that if Owens was convicted of any offense, he would immediately agree to resign. The agreement was to last for one year.

After this agreement had been in force for about three months, the state Child Support Recovery Unit notified Darby Owens that his wages would be garnished because of unpaid child support. According to Darby Owens, the garnishment notice was "the straw that broke the camel's back." The next day Darby Owens orally submitted his resignation to the assistant chief, stating "I can't do this anymore." Darby Owens turned in his badge, identification, name plate, and the keys to his office and car. Four days later, Darby Owens sought to withdraw his resignation; however, Tory Huntsman refused to permit him to withdraw his resignation.

Pursuant to state law pertaining to the removal, suspension, and demotion of deputy sheriffs, Darby Owens wrote the Woodbury County Civil Service Commission (CSC) requesting a hearing regarding the circumstances surrounding his termination and resignation from the sheriff's department.   In this proceeding, Darby Owens was the complainant and Tory Huntsman was the respondent. The CSC held the hearing and allowed each party to present its respective position.

Darby Owens argued before the CSC that he had been constructively discharged, claiming that the following chain of events caused him to resign: (1) Tory Huntsman, acting on his own, and without authority from the county, instituted a criminal investigation against him; (2) the investigation led to the filing of criminal charges against him; (3) the criminal proceedings cost him thousands of dollars to defend; (4) during a portion of the proceedings, Tory Huntsman placed him on paid suspension, during which time he was not allowed to engage in off-duty law enforcement work; (5) as a condition of returning to work after the criminal proceedings, he agreed to a 30-day unpaid suspension; (6) when he returned to work, he was assigned to an administrative position for which he had no experience; (7) all these incidents led to increased stress and financial problems; and (8) in time, these incidents caused him to fail to pay his child support and to resign after he was notified that his wages would be garnished. Darby Owens also contended that he had attempted to withdraw his resignation, but Tory Huntsman had refused to allow him to do so, even though Tory Huntsman had allowed other personnel to withdraw their resignations.

The CSC found that Darby Owens had "voluntarily resigned his deputy sheriff's position solely as a result of his wages having been garnished and that no action on the part of the Sheriff's Department constituted harassment or placed any undue pressure or stress upon ... Owens to resign so as to constitute a termination or removal." This finding was affirmed on appeal to the state trial court, the court of appeals and the State supreme court.

Thereafter, Darby Owens filed a complaint in the proper federal district court, against Woodbury County alleging that Tory Huntsman, an employee of Woodbury County, had retaliated against him in violation of federal law because of Owens opposition to Huntsman in a prior Sheriff's election. Owens also alleged that he was constructively discharged by the County, through Sheriff Huntsman, asserting the same eight arguments on the constructive discharge issue that he had asserted against Huntsman before the CSC, the state district court, and the Connecticut Supreme Court.

Woodbury County has moved for summary judgment.

Questions

1.   Assume that part of the county's motion for summary judgment alleges that the entire claim is barred by claim preclusion. Why should this argument be rejected?

2. The county also claims that issues of constructive discharge have been resolved and those issues are precluded.

A. First, the county says that Tory Huntsman and the County are in privity and that the judgment in favor of Huntsman should operate as a judgment in favor of the County on these issues. What result? Why?

B. Second, the county claims that it can use "Defensive" claim preclusion to foreclose Huntsman from relitigating the constructive discharge issue? Discuss.

Chapter 11

Appeals

Who May Appeal? "Aggrieved Parties"

Evans v. Alpha Sigma Nu Sorority of Sisters, Inc.

Return to the facts of this problem in Chapter 6 under Necessary/Indispensable parties.

Assume that the IntraSorority Council (ISC) of Western Kentucky Wesleyan University, is the campus organization that regulates all sororities on the campus, and of which the local Alpha Sigma Nu Sorority is a member. Because of recent allegations of abuse of alcohol by members of the Greek communities, the ISC has adopted new regulations effective with the current school term. If any member sorority, or any of its sisters, is found, in any action, civil or criminal, to have abused alcohol, the sorority would be suspended from all campus activities for the balance of the semester.

Sara Barnhart is the president of the Western Kentucky Wesleyan chapter of Alpa Sigma Nu. When the action is filed by Rhonda

Evans, Barnhard is aware that a substantial portion of the underlying complaint involves allegations that the chapter's sisters were abusing alcohol and that it was that abuse that produced the noise levels of which Evans complains.

Questions

1. Not wanting to get the chapter directly involved, Sara Barnhart recommends to her executive committee that the chapter monitor the suit against the alumnae corporation. When the *Evans v. Alpha Sigma Nu Sorority of Sisters, Inc.* was tried in state court, Evans was successful in having the property declared a nuisance, based on the noise and alcohol abuse facts shown at trial. The local chapter now seeks to appeal the trial court verdict alleging that if it sought to do so, it would have been permitted to intervene under Rule 24(a) and, because its interest lost at trial, it should be allowed to appeal. What result? Why?

2. Assume instead that Sara Barnhart and the local chapter seek to intervene in the underlying action prior to trial under Rule 24(a). They do so because the underlying facts of the case allege alcohol abuse by the current chapter and because of the impact of any adverse ruling on the local chapter's ability to continue. The trial court denies the local chapter's intervention motion. Can the local chapter appeal that ruling? Why or why not? When should such an appeal be filed?

3. When the local chapter is not allowed to intervene, do they now have the right to appeal the judgment in the underlying proceeding?

McWilliams v. DelMonte Hotels, Inc.

Andre McWilliams was a citizen of New Jersey employed as a driver for Columbus Hotels, Inc., at Delaware corporation at one of the large metropolitan New York airports. McWilliams was seriously injured when struck by another airport van, this one owned by DelMonte Hotels, Inc., a New York corporation and being driven by Steven Abrams, a citizen of New York. One of the allegations in the subsequent investigation was that DelMonte driver Abrams was intoxicated at the time of the accident. Andre McWilliams subsequently died from his injuries. Loraine McWilliams, Andre's wife, filed a wrongful death action against DelMonte and Abrams in the appropriate federal district court on the basis of diversity.

After extensive negotiation, the insurance company for DelMonte agreed to pay $500,000 to the McWilliams estate in full settlement of the claim. In addition, the personal insurance company for Abrams agreed to pay Abrams' policy limit of $50,000 direct to DelMonte as contribution. Upon motion by Abrams for judgment in this fashion, a motion to which DelMonte consented, the trial court entered judgment in favor of plaintiffs as described. When, however, this settlement was discussed at the board of directors meeting of DelMonte Hotels, Inc., the board was furious that Abrams was not required to pay monies personally since the accident was almost exclusively his fault.

Questions

1. Is DelMonte Hotels, Inc. an "aggrieved" party as a result of the facts in this problem?

2. Can DelMonte Hotels, Inc. file an appeal of the $500,000 judgment against it? Why or why not?

Masterson v. Likking & the City of Dodge

Darlene Masterson, a citizen of Colorado was injured when she tripped on the sidewalk in front of Marianna Likking's house on Tradd Street in Dodge City, Kansas. Masterson sued Likking, a Kansas citizen and Dodge City, a Kansas municipal corporation in an appropriate federal court on the basis of diversity alleging they were both negligent and jointly and severally liable for her injuries. Masterson, who was visiting a friend in Dodge City, alleged that she tripped and injured herself when she accidentally inserted her foot into a hole where the sidewalk abutted an old coal grate outside Likking's house. The grate is a textured piece of sheet metal covering an opening in the sidewalk which historically was a chute for coal to be delivered into the basement of the house. The opening is reinforced with brick, and the sidewalk is concrete. Counsel for Marianna Likking filed a motion for summary judgment arguing that the facts revealed that a defect in the sidewalk, not a problem with the coal grate, caused Masterson's fall. Likking noted that, as a matter of law, Dodge City was responsible for maintaining the public sidewalk, and in fact, "Dodge City has admitted this responsibility...." In opposition, the City asserted that it did not own the steel grate or the brick shaft and was not the responsible party. The trial court granted Likking summary judgment and found that the hole in which Masterson tripped was part of the sidewalk. In its conclusions of law, the trial court continued:

> There is no evidence in the record which would create a material question of fact that Likking owed a duty to inspect and maintain *public sidewalks* outside her house. The evidence in the record, taken in the light most favorable to the Plaintiff, establishes that even if Likking had some ownership rights in the air shaft cover and its surrounding stone, such structures were squarely upon the public sidewalk and subject to the Dodge City's control.

The City has appealed the grant of summary judgment in favor of Likking.

Question

Is Dodge City an "aggrieved party" with a right to appeal a decision in favor of a codefendant granting it summary judgment and dismissing it from a case filed by a plaintiff?

Who May Appeal? Mootness

Braverwood Development Co. v. Peterson

Gerald and Darlene Peterson, citizens of Nevada, agreed to sell a large tract of realty to Braverwood Development Co., a Texas corporation. The property itself was in Nevada. Braverwood had designs to put a casino/spa on the property. The Petersons breached the sales agreement by refusing to convey the property to Braverwood at the closing. Braverwood filed a federal court lawsuit, based on diversity of citizenship, against the Petersons alleging several causes of action, including specific performance, breach of contract, tortious interference, declaratory judgment, and breach of constructive trust. The Petersons filed motions and appeared *pro se* at each hearing scheduled regarding the litigation. About a year after the suit was filed, the trial court granted summary judgment in favor of Braverwood Development Co. and ordered the Petersons to convey the property. When the Petersons failed to do so, Braverwood filed a motion seeking to hold the Petersons in contempt. The Petersons appeared at the contempt hearing and asked that the matter be continued so they could obtain counsel, a motion the court denied. The court then advised the Petersons of the consequences of being found in contempt. Later that same day, the Petersons conveyed the contested property to Braverwood in exchange for $565,000.00. The Petersons now appeal, claiming the trial court should have granted their motion for continuance. They also argue that summary judgment was too harsh a remedy and that they should not be required, under the law, to convey the property.

Questions

1. Did the Petersons do anything inconsistent with an attempt to appeal? What?
2. How should the appellate court handle the actions of the Petersons? Why?

"Final Orders" Subject to Appeal

Farr v. Martin, et als.

Tyson Farr was a citizen of Arkansas. While visiting friends in Memphis, Tennessee, Farr's car wound up in front of a vehicle driven by Derek Martin, in which Angela Fowler was a passenger. Martin and Fowler were suspects in a recent bank robbery and were being pursued by police officers David Stuart and Harrison Mencken, both of whom were officers in Memphis. During the chase, the car being driven by Martin struck Tyson Farr's car, killing him.

In response, Tyson Farr's mother, Jolina Farr, filed suit in a proper federal district court for wrongful death against Derek Martin, Angela Fowler, David Stuart, Harrison Mencken and the City of Memphis. Without answering, Stuart, Mencken and the City moved for summary judgment alleging that they were immune from suit because they were acting within the scope of their official duties as a local government and government officers. The court granted this motion and Jolina Farr appeals the grant of summary judgment.

Questions

1. Is the judgment in favor of Stuart, Mencken and the City of Memphis "final" as to them?

2. Is it a "final order" for purposes of appeal? Why or why not?

3. If you determined that the order granting summary judgment was not a "final order" for purposes of appeal, is there any way to make it so?

Haass v. Metropolitan Transit, Inc.

Yvonne Haass is a citizen of Wisconsin who was visiting Rockford, Illinois when she rode on a bus owned and operated by Metropolitan Transit, Inc., an Illinois corporation. At some point while on her bus trip, Yvonne Haass fell to the floor of the bus and was injured. She filed a *pro se* lawsuit in an appropriate federal district court alleging diversity of citizenship and damages in excess of $75,000. Her rambling *pro se* complaint, however, made little sense and, upon motion made under Rule 12(b)(6) by Metropolitan Transit, the court dismissed the complaint for failure to state a claim. Yvonne then filed a notice of appeal.

Questions

1. Does the granting of the motion under Rule 12(b)(6) dispose of the case? Is the order final?
2. Is the dismissal a "final order" for purpose of appeal?
3. Can you think of a factual circumstance under which the 12(b)(6) dismissal could be a "final order" for appeal purposes?

Sulky Trucks North America, Inc. v. Hanson, et als.

Erick Hanson was a citizen of Nebraska who wanted to get into the business of selling automobiles and trucks. He created several related automobile dealership companies. As the dealerships grew, he would form new companies, most of which included the words "Truck Heaven" somewhere in the name and listed him as sole or majority shareholder. At some point, these companies began dealing vehicles purchased from Sulky Trucks North America, Inc. (Sulky), a corporate citizen of Delaware, and were initially successful in doing so, handling approximately ten percent of all Sulky's sales in the United States. As a result, and at Sulky's behest, Hanson and his companies began purchasing large quantities of vehicles from Sulky at a substantial discount. As he continued to expand his Sulky dealerships, Hanson acted as guarantor of certain debts and obligations of the dealerships. At some point, the relationship soured as Hanson came to distrust Sulky and Sulky believed that Hanson and Truck Heaven businesses were grossly overextended in the market. It was at this point that Sulky filed suit in a proper federal district court against Hanson, Truck Heaven Companies, and related parties over an alleged breach of a $1.3 million loan agreement. Hanson and Truck Heaven Companies responded by filing their own claims against Sulky and Sulky Finance based on conduct surrounding the loan agreement and other alleged wrongful acts. In their counterclaim, Hanson alleged violations of the federal Auto Dealers' Day in Court act, an act designed to regulate franchise arrangements between car dealers and manufacturers; breach of contract, fraud, constructive fraud, and misrepresentation.

In a Rule 12(b)(6) ruling, the district court dismissed Hanson's action under the Auto Dealer's Day in Court act. The court also granted summary judgment in favor of Sulky on its loan default claim. The court also granted summary judgment against Hanson on the fraud and misrepresentation claim. At this point, Hanson appealed the rulings of the district court.

Questions

1. Is the action "final" for purposes of appeal? Why or why not?
2. Suppose, after the notice of appeal is filed, Hanson and Sulky

enter into a stipulation in the trial court which 1.) Dismissed the constructive fraud claim by Hanson against Sulky, 2.) Allowed Hanson a setoff of $500,000 against the loan default on the misrepresentation claim and 3.) Indicated that all other issues among the parties are resolved. Does that change your answer to question 1 in any way? How?

Interlocutory Appeals

Injunctions

Solomon v. New York State Board of Elections

Margarite Solomon is a citizen of New York, a lawyer, a Civil Court judge in one of New York City's five boroughs, and a would-be candidate for state Supreme Court Justice. In New York, a supreme court justice is a trial court judge. They are chosen in popular election and run on a party slate, generally on either the Republican or Democratic ticket. In place in New York is a complex system whereby individuals are nominated for political positions. To be nominated, a would-be candidate must assemble a substantial group of delegates who would participate in the party nominating process. Margarite Solomon has filed a federal lawsuit in a correct federal district court alleging that the complicated nominating process violates her federal civil rights claiming that New York's electoral scheme violates the First and Fourteenth Amendments to the U.S. Constitution. Solomon alleged that the New York electoral system violates the First Amendment's guarantee of political association as to Supreme Court Justice candidates and the voters wishing to support them. Plaintiffs also claim that the scheme violates the Equal Protection Clause of the Fourteenth Amendment because it places unequal burdens on the right to vote. Solomon sought a declaration that the provisions of state law providing for the challenged electoral scheme is unconstitutional. She also sought an injunction requiring the State Legislature to enact a new election scheme, and in the meantime requiring the State to conduct direct primary elections for the office of Supreme Court Justice. The District Court granted numerous motions to intervene, including one filed by the State Attorney General. When Solomon moved for a preliminary injunction seeking to enjoin the current electoral process until a final hearing on the merits, the District Court conducted a hearing and issued a Memorandum and Order granting plaintiffs' motion on First Amendment grounds without considering plaintiffs' equal protection claim. The Court thus enjoined defendants from enforcing the contested election law pending a final hearing and ordered that the State conduct primary elections for the office of Supreme Court Justice until the Legislature enacts a new election scheme. The Board of Elections appealed this order.

Questions

1. Upon the issuance of a preliminary injunction, has the case concluded? That is, is the injunction a Final Order in the case?
2. If it is not a final order, how can it be appealed? Why is an appeal particularly appropriate, procedurally, in a case such as this?

Arthur's Furniture Masterpieces, Inc. v. Al's Furniture Barn, Inc.

Arthur's Furniture Masterpieces, Inc. is a Delaware corporation specializing in "high-end" original furniture designs. Arthur's designer derived nearly all of the design elements of the company's Grand Inheritance and English Manor furniture collections from the public domain, using mainly eighteenth and nineteenth century designs. Following this design, Arthur's Furniture Masterpieces, Inc. obtained Certificates of Registration from the U.S. Copyright Office for these collections, which covered "decorative sculptural designs on furniture; adaptation of preexisting decorative designs; compilation of decorative designs on suites of furniture."

Al's Furniture Barn, Inc. is a Montana corporation which markets lower-cost furniture modeled after existing furniture designs. In fact, Arthur's Furniture Masterpieces, Inc. discovered that Al's Furniture Barn, Inc..'s 20200 collection displayed pieces from Arthur's Furniture Masterpieces, Inc.'s English Manor collection. Al's Furniture Barn, Inc. also showcased a 20000 collection that Arthur's Furniture Masterpieces, Inc. claims was strikingly similar to its Grand Inheritance collection. Al's Furniture Barn, Inc. concedes it intended to sell pieces substantially similar to Arthur's Furniture Masterpieces, Inc.'s two collections before becoming aware that the collections were copyrighted.

To avoid a copyright infringement suit, Al's Furniture Barn, Inc. agreed with Arthur's Furniture Masterpieces, Inc. not to develop or market its 20000 and 20200 collections. Thereafter, Al's Furniture Barn, Inc.. redesigned its 20000 and 20200 collections. When Al's Furniture Barn, Inc. began marketing its redesigned collections, it was clear to Arthur's Furniture Masterpieces that although Al's Furniture Barn, Inc.'s designer changed various sculptural features and design elements, the redesigned collections was still substantially similar to its copyrighted English Manor and Grand Inheritance collections. Accordingly, Arthur's Furniture Masterpieces, Inc.'s filed a copyright infringement suit in the proper federal district court and moved for a preliminary injunction barring Al's Furniture Barn, Inc.'s promotion and sale of the 20000 and 20200 collections. Al's Furniture Barn, Inc.

answered and opposed the motion. In denying a preliminary injunction, the district court determined that the balance of hardships stood in equipoise and that Arthur's Furniture Masterpieces, therefore, had to demonstrate a stronger probability of success than if the balance had tipped in its favor. Based on the sparse record available at the preliminary stage of litigation, the court concluded that the validity of Arthur's copyrights was questionable, at least insofar as the copyrights concerned Arthur's compilations of adapted public-domain designs.

Arthur's Furniture Masterpieces, Inc. appeals the denial of preliminary injunctive relief.

Questions

1. Upon the denial of a preliminary injunction, has the case concluded? That is, is the injunction a Final Order in the case?

2. If it is not a final order, how can it be appealed? Is an appeal appropriate, procedurally, in a case such as this?

Controlling Questions of Law

Ernesto Cruz, M.D, v. Community Hospital, Inc.

Dr. Ernesto Cruz is a native of Mexico but is licensed in the United States as an obstetrician-gynecologist who was granted medical staff membership and clinical privileges at Community Hospital During a laparoscopic procedure on a patient at Community Hospital, Cruz inadvertently punctured the iliac artery of the patient, creating a life-threatening emergency. Cruz states that this is a known possible complication of the procedure. Following a lengthy series of proceedings, Community suspended Cruz's staff membership and clinical privileges. Community Hospital then conducted a "Peer Review" of all cases in which Cruz had been the primary care physician for a period of two years. The committee conducting the "Peer Review" found 24 of the 102 cases to be problematic. Based on the Committee's report, Community suspended Cruz's privileges, pending a review by Community's Medical Board. At Cruz's request, the Hearing Committee of the Medical Board, which is composed of three physicians, conducted a full hearing and, following that hearing, the Medical Board voted to terminate Cruz's medical staff privileges. Community's Board of Trustee's upheld that decision.

Dr. Cruz filed an action against Community Hospital in an appropriate federal district court alleging that the termination of his privileges constituted discrimination against him on the basis of his race and national origin, in violation his federal civil rights. He further alleged that the hospital performed its medical peer review functions in a discriminatory manner, treating non-Mexican physicians differently and disciplining them less harshly. During discovery, Cruz sought to obtain all peer review records related to all reviews of physicians for any reason, during the twenty years preceding his request. Community Hospital sought a protective order, arguing that the peer review materials were privileged under state law. Cruz filed a motion to compel production of the materials. The district court refused to recognize a privilege for medical peer review materials and denied Community's motion for protective order. The court, however, certified this order for interlocutory appeal.

Questions

1. Is this case Final, for purposes of appeal?
2. What does the court mean when it: "certified this order for interlocutory appeal?" Where is such a process authorized?

Non-Statutory Interlocutory Appeals--
Collateral Order Doctrine

Gehlhorn v. Callahan

Anthony J. Gehlhorn was formerly an inmate confined to a federal correctional facility in Louisiana. Dr. Larry Callahan was a staff physician working at the correctional facility during Gehlhorn's term of imprisonment. While on work release as a "hopper" on a garbage collection truck, Gehlhorn's right leg was crushed below the knee when the truck collided with another vehicle. He underwent immediate surgery and initial recovery at a local hospital. The treating physician ultimately discharged Gehlhorn indicating that Gehlhorn should continue antibiotic treatment and wound cleansing and that he should have periodic visits with an orthopedic specialist. Later, Gehlhorn was admitted into the 24-Hour Unit at the prison infirmary due to the risk of infection. Dr. Callahan, Gehlhorn's primary physician, personally examined Gehlhorn on three occasions during the span of two and one half months, and apparently issued orders on nine occasions. Despite this treatment, Gehlhorn complained of wound related discomfort or apprehension concerning the care of his leg on five occasions. When Gehlhorn was released from prison, he sought private medical treatment. He was diagnosed with osteomyelitis in his injured leg. Osteomyelitis is an inflamation of the bone marrow often caused by a bacterial infection. This condition required multiple corrective surgeries.

Gehlhorn filed suit in an appropriate federal district court alleging that Dr. Callahan's failure to treat his injured and infected leg constituted a violation of his Eighth Amendment right to medical treatment for serious medical need. Dr. Callahan asserted, by way of affirmative defense, qualified immunity. Qualified immunity provides government officials performing discretionary functions with a shield against civil damages liability, so long as their actions could reasonably have been thought consistent with the rights they are alleged to have violated. Dr. Callahan then moved for summary judgment which the district court denied. Dr. Callahan has appealed that denial.

Questions

1. Is the case Final for appeal purposes? That is, is the denial of a motion for summary judgment a "final order?"
2. If it is not final, how does Dr. Callahan have an ability to appeal the denial of summary judgment?

Standard of Review

Generally

Fenwick v. Matlock Financial Services, Inc.

Lilian Fenwick, a citizen of New Hampshire, was employed by Matlock Financial Services, Inc., a Delaware corporation. Fenwick also suffered from Obsessive Compulsive Disorder (OCD), and, while employed by Matloc k Financial Services, she experienced an OCD "episode." Fenwick visited a doctor, who recommended restrictions on her work conditions, including frequent breaks and no changes in work assignments. Matlock Financial Services determined that it was unable to accommodate the proposed restrictions, and it therefore did not allow Fenwick to return to work. Five months after the episode, Fenwick's health improved and her doctor recommended less stringent restrictions on Fenwick's work conditions. Matlock Financial Services allowed Fenwick to return to work. During her five-month absence, Fenwick continued to receive her salary by using accumulated sick leave. Despite returning to work, Fenwick brought suit against Matlock Financial Services, in an appropriate federal district court, asserting causes of action under the federal Americans with Disabilities Act and the federal Family and Medical Leave Act. Fenwick claimed Matlock Financial Services's delay in allowing her to return to work constituted unlawful discrimination and retaliation within the meaning of these statutes. The case went to trial, and the jury rendered a verdict in favor of Matlock Financial Services. Lilian Fenwick has appealed the adverse judgment claiming that the District Court committed reversible error.

Questions

1. Lillian Fenwick first claims that the District Court incorrectly instructed the jury on the law, noting that a United States Supreme Court case handed down just prior to the trial of her action changed the measure of damages in her action and that the trial court instead instructed on the former standard. What standard will the court of appeals use to review this claim.

2. Lillian Fenwich also claims that the district court erred during jury selection; first in striking for cause a hearing-impaired juror rather than accommodating her disability; and second, in striking for cause a juror who had been a teacher of Fenwick's counsel's legal assistant. As to the hearing-impaired potential juror, during *voir dire,* the juror in question stated that she had always wanted to serve on a jury but that she had a ringing in her ears and could not hear people when they turned around or lowered their voices. The District Judge asked the juror if moving her to the front row would enable her to hear the proceedings, to which she responded in the negative. The juror had to ask the District Judge to repeat himself during *voir dire* because, despite the fact that the District Judge was only three or four feet away, she had difficulty hearing him. The juror also stated that she had never used a hearing aid, characterizing herself as "stubborn about it." As to the teacher, the person was a former professor to the legal assistant of Fenwick's lawyer. In addition, the professor disclosed during *voir dire* that he believed an employer had discriminated against him in the past and that his wife had once been precluded from employment for a time because of a disability; as a result of these experiences, the professor expressed some uncertainty as to his ability to consider the case without bias. What standard will the court of appeals use to review these two claims? Suppose the judges on the court of appeals each agree that they would not have struck the hearing-impaired juror?

3. Finally, Lillian Fenwick claims error in the jury instructions. The trial court instructed the jury as follows: "To recover against Matlock Financial Services for retaliation, Ms. Fenwick has the burden of proving all of the elements as follows: That she was qualified to perform the job, that she was subjected to an adverse employment action at that time or after the protected conduct took place[,][a]nd that Matlock Financial Services took adverse employment action because she engaged in the protected conduct." Fenwick did not object to this instruction at trial, but you may assume that the law is that an ADA plaintiff need not establish that she was qualified to perform her job in order to recover on a retaliation claim. What standard will the court of appeals use to review this claim?

Review of Facts

Estate of O'Shaunnessey v. Cascade State University

Matthew O'Shaunnessey, a citizen of North Dakota, was employed for many years as a Professor in the Political Science Department of Cascade State University, a North Dakota corporation. The university provided to all employees, including O'Shaunnessey, a group benefits plan that provided, among other things, a basic life, accidental death and dismemberment benefit of $20,000. In addition, Matthew elected supplemental life insurance coverage for $166,000--three times his annual salary.

Matthew O'Shaunnessey died of a heart attack, having left his wife Catherine as his designated first beneficiary. The beneficiary designation form on file with the University's Employee Benefits Office listed Catherine as receiving 100% of the insurance benefits. In addition, the form also listed O'Shaunnessey's brother Lewis, whose name appeared on the form below Catherine's, as also receiving 100%. Matthew indicated on the form that if neither Catherine nor Lewis were living or eligible when the insurance proceeds were to be paid out, then 100% of the proceeds were to go to the scholarship fund of the Political Science Department. Following notification of his death, the Employee Benefits Office of the university informed Catherine that it was approving her claim for the group life insurance benefits and was depositing $194,640.35 in a security money market account created in her name in accordance with the policy provisions. Shortly thereafter, however, the Employee Benefits Office received an unexpected call from Lewis averring that it had been his brother's intention for Catherine and he to split the insurance proceeds. The Employee Benefits Office explained the details of Raymond's beneficiary designation form and told Lewis that Catherine would be the beneficiary of 100% of the insurance proceeds. The Employee Benefits Office further explained with a copy of the policy provisions with respect to changing beneficiaries and explained that Raymond had not changed his beneficiary designation at any time from Catherine to Lewis or expressed an intention for Catherine or Lewis to divide the insurance proceeds.

Shortly thereafter, Lewis, a citizen of Colorado, filed suit in an appropriate federal district court against Cascade State University and Catherine O'Shaunnessey. In the suit, Lewis sought to be declared a beneficiary under the group life insurance policy. He claimed entitlement to one-half of the insurance benefits due upon Raymond's death.

Neither party requested a jury and the district court issued a ruling in Cascade State's favor dismissing Lewis's claims. It held that the plan administrator had made a factual determination and that the plan administrator's decision was not arbitrary or capricious, as there was concrete evidence in the record to support the decision that Lewis is not eligible for benefits under the plan.

Questions

1. What standard will the court of appeals use to review this appeal? Why?
2. What is the likely result?

Plain Error

Capeon v. New Age Realty, Inc

Joyce Capeon is a citizen of Michigan and was employed as a real estate sales agent by New Age Realty, Inc., a Michigan corporate citizen.

Capeon filed suit in an appropriate federal district court alleging that New Age Realty, Inc. discriminated against her on the basis of sex when it set her level of compensation for various real estate related activities, in violation of federal law.

The case was tried to a jury, Evidence revealed that Joyce Capeon's compensation package was set at approximately $20,000 less per year then her male counterparts. At the conclusion of the evidence, the trial judge instructed the jury on the law related to sex discrimination and the way in which the jury could find damages, if it was so inclined. There were no objections to the jury instructions. The jury found in favor of Joyce Capeon and awarded her $120,000 in damages.

On appeal, New Age Realty argues that the trial court erred in instructing the jury in that the instructions should have included a statement that the maximum period for which back pay damages are available under federal law is two years.

Questions

1. What standard will the court of appeals use to determine this issue? Why?
2. What result?